Karen Holland

Buying a Computer for Seniors

in
easy steps

For the Over 50s

In easy steps is an imprint of In Easy Steps Limited
Southfield Road · Southam
Warwickshire CV47 0FB · United Kingdom
www.ineasysteps.com

Notice of Liability
Every effort has been made to ensure that this book contains accurate
and current information. However, In Easy Steps Limited and the
author shall not be liable for any loss or damage suffered by readers
as a result of any information contained herein.

Trademarks
All trademarks are acknowledged as belonging to their respective
companies.

In Easy Steps Limited supports The Forest Stewardship Council (FSC),
the leading international forest certification organisation. All our titles
that are printed on Greenpeace approved FSC certified paper carry the
FSC logo.

Mixed Sources
Product group from well-managed
forests and other controlled sources
www.fsc.org Cert no. SGS-COC-005998
© 1996 Forest Stewardship Council

Printed and bound in the United Kingdom

ISBN 978-1-84078-368-1

Contents

1 Before You Start

This chapter outlines everything that's in this book. It tells you how to get started on the task of buying your computer.

Seniors and Computers

Research shows that using a computer as you get older can help keep your brain active for longer. And that's in addition to other time- and energy- saving benefits. You can use a computer to:

● Communicate with friends and family

● Manage your finances

● Research and pursue your hobbies

● Book holidays or do shopping without leaving the house

● and much, much more...

Some people believe that computers are the domain of the young. But an increasing number of seniors are successfully using computers on a daily basis. In 2005, one quarter of people aged 70–75 used a computer online, and this has already significantly increased to 45 percent.

Some examples of real senior computer users include:

● An 88-year old British grandmother who uses her laptop to communicate with her daughter and grandchildren by email after they emigrated to the US

● A 68-year old who manages the administration of his local retired-professionals society using spreadsheets and word-processing packages

● A 66-year old who used social networking sites on the Internet recently to get back in touch with old friends she hadn't had contact with since leaving school all those years ago

● A 64-year old who uses his computer to manage his extensive photography collection and create DVDs of family occasions from video-camera footage

Don't forget

You don't have to learn on your own. Computers can be complex, however there are plenty of local training sessions and computer clubs you can join, many aimed specifically at seniors. Start by looking at your local adult education service.

Using This Book

You obviously don't have to buy a computer to use one or use the Internet. You can go to a local library or other institution and rent one. But while this gets you access to a computer for short periods of time, it doesn't bring you very many of the benefits of owning a computer.

This book explains why seniors in particular can benefit from having their own computer, how to simplify the process of buying one, and where to start!

This book is a guide to the computer buying process in easy steps, from identifying your needs, to choosing and buying a computer, and supporting it once you've got it home.

Coping with technology

As with all consumer technology, computers change and progress at an alarming rate. You may have bought computers for your children when they were younger, or have used computers in your workplace, but computers of today are very different.

You may need to learn some new techniques, however, technological advances are generally an advantage:

- Firstly, computers, components and peripherals (such as printers, scanners, web cameras etc) are cheaper than ever to buy – you don't need to spend as much to get connected.

- Secondly, each new generation of computer gets easier to use. Gone are the days when you needed to understand how a computer worked in order to run it.

If you have the inclination, you can use a computer, regardless of your age or previous experience.

Don't be put off by the large range of computers available, or the fact that you can buy them almost anywhere (including your local supermarket). This book will help you narrow down the options, while ensuring that you get what's right for you.

Hot tip

Don't be tempted to wait for newer technology to come out, or prices to go down. This is a continual process and you'll be waiting forever!

This Book Isn't...

This book is not a pricing manual or component buying guide. It doesn't contain specific prices for computers, or the names or costs of individual components.

There are several reasons for this:

● Details of components and their prices change as often as the technology does, and this can be as much as weekly!

● There are so many different suppliers it would be impossible to include them all

● Price and availability, of computers and components, varies considerably depending on where you live

Similarly, there is an ever increasing number of places to buy a computer, as existing shops diversify their sales lines, and as more commerce is done over the Internet.

What this book does

This book gives you the background and information you need to be able to make decisions for yourself.

It also gives you information about other places you can go to get that detailed and regularly updated information, both in person and using the Internet.

Hot tip

The Internet is the best place to go for the latest information about computer makes and models. There are lots of websites, updated by different people and companies. Read on for information.

The Buying Process

When you're making any purchase, you go through a number of decisions, collectively known as the buying process. It works as follows:

Hot tip

The time you spend researching what to buy is really valuable, otherwise you risk buying a computer that won't be able to do everything you want it to.

This process is very useful for reminding us to get all the information we need before we buy something. This is particularly appropriate for high value purchases like a computer:

- Unless you understand what you'll be using it for, how can you buy something that will meet your needs?

- If you don't research and evaluate information about all the options, how can you be sure that you're making the right decision?

- Once you've made the purchase, did you make the right decision – should you go elsewhere in future?

Chapter Overviews

Your requirements

The first part of this book is about understanding computers and what they can mean for you:

- **Computing for Seniors** (Chapter 2) shows you possibilities you may not have previously considered, using the common practices of other senior users. It shows you that how you use your computer affects what you should buy and how much you spend on it

Learning about computers

These chapters give you an overview of the different components and technologies that make up a computer, as well as describing all the different types of computer currently available.

It also gives you information about the other activities you'll need to address but may not have thought about, for example, how to get Internet access for your computer:

- **Inside a Computer** (Chapter 3) teaches you about the key internal components of a computer. It explains which elements are worth knowing about and why

- **Peripherals** (Chapter 4) explains what common external components should be part of your purchase plan, including items that are particularly designed for senior computer users

- **Choose Your Type** (Chapter 5) helps you decide if you want a desktop, laptop or netbook, and whether to opt for Windows, Mac or something else. It describes each type, including its space and power requirements and other differences

- **Software** (Chapter 6) explains what software you'll need, and whether it comes with the computer. It tells you about the market leaders, including free or cheaper alternatives where possible

- **Networking** (Chapter 7) explains what you need to link your computer and peripherals together, and how to connect to the Internet

Deciding what to buy

This part of the book helps you to put all of the information you've gathered into perspective, so that you can make decisions about what computer to buy, and where to buy it from:

Making a decision

- **Buy The Right Thing** (Chapter 8) uses a set of questions to help you match your specific requirements to the right computer for you

- **Where to Buy** (Chapter 9) provides you with information about the different methods you can use and places you can go to purchase your computer

Life after your purchase

The chapters in this section cover all the tasks you'll need to look at once you've bought the computer of your dreams!

Post-purchase evaluation

- **Getting Set Up** (Chapter 10) looks at the practical aspects of using a computer, including guidance on positioning your equipment, and the regular activities you should plan as soon as you get your computer home, for example backing up your data

- **Going Mobile** (Chapter 11) is an additional chapter that covers the use of handheld mobile devices, such as a mobile phone, and how to incorporate them into your home computing setup

13

Hot tip

This part of the book helps you decide which computer to buy and the essentials you'll need to do to set it up.

Finding Out More

This book gives you an overview of computers and how to use them as well as information about the different things you can do, for example with access to the Internet.

It also gives you a glossary of the key terms you'll need to know: see Chapter 12.

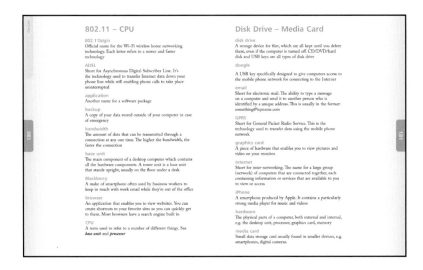

If you want further information there are a number of places you can go, including:

- **Local library**. You'll find a number of resources here: a wide range of books about all the different aspects of computing. There are guides including learning about using different software packages

- **Website directory.** Addresses of websites where you can find more information about technology or online shopping sites

- **Other resources**. Other training and information resources specifically written or designed for seniors. We cover more of these in Chapter 2 (Computing for Seniors) and Chapter 8 (Buy The Right Thing)

2 Computing for Seniors

Computers can be incredibly useful things, regardless of your age. But as a senior, a computer enables you to really take it easy. Use it to order shopping for home delivery, for writing emails and letters to friends and family, and for keeping up with your hobbies.

Why You Need a Computer

Computers can be brilliant time- and energy-saving devices for everyone, but they can be particularly useful for seniors.

Having a computer enables you to:

- Reduce the effort and cost of keeping in touch with friends and family

- Save time and effort around the house and in your everyday life

- Better manage your photos and other documents

- Bring your interests and hobbies to you, without having to leave the house!

Think before you buy

Before you buy a computer you should think carefully about what you'll be using it for. Some of the options may require you to pick a more powerful computer or to choose slightly different or more advanced components.

If you are going to be manipulating images, for example editing home videos or recording television programs, then you will need a more powerful computer.

If you are planning to simply use a word processor to write shopping lists, or use email to keep in touch with friends then you won't require the same level of power or sophistication in a computer.

You are probably already aware of the basic uses for a computer, but don't skip this chapter – you may find other uses for your new purchase that you hadn't previously considered.

Planning ahead will ensure you get a computer that will last you as long as possible.

Beware

If you already have access to the Internet, there are lots of places online where you can learn more about the things discussed in this chapter. See Page 14 for some suggested places to start.

Communicate by Email

Email (an abbreviation of electronic mail) is now one of the most commonly used applications on a computer. It enables you to send a message to anyone with an email address, which they receive almost instantly, regardless of where they are in the world.

As an older person, you may find it easier to use email than handwriting letters in order to:

- **Keep in touch with friends and family in far away places.** Email is generally quicker, cheaper and more reliable than the local postal service

- **Send or receive pictures or documents**. This is a favorite with people wanting regular updates on how things are growing (either grandchildren or plants depending on your family and interests)

- **Send newsletter-style updates to friends and family.** You can send the same email to multiple people at the same time

- **Reduce the repetition in personal communications.** You can save time and energy because you keep a copy of everything that is sent out, so it's easy to re-use text without having to re-write it

Don't forget

It's becoming more common for businesses to use email too, which saves money on calls. However, not all companies respond as quickly to emails as phone calls. So you should still consider calling for important matters.

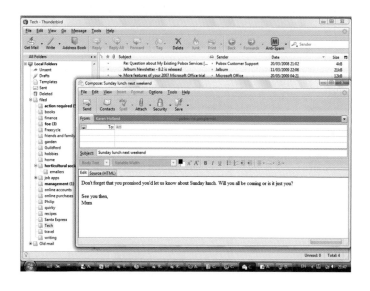

Visiting the Internet

The Internet has a number of different names – the World Wide Web, or Web, but they all refer to the same thing – a giant network of computers and servers linked together. Your computer connects to the network to view and "download" information.

"Surfing" or "browsing" the Internet simply means using a computer program (an Internet browser) to view the information that other people have made available on their websites. Once you've got a computer you can use websites for the following:

- **Finding information**. Some sites provide you with information and usually save you having to call or go somewhere. Examples include your local council, National Rail (train timetables) and retailers' websites

- **Making online purchases.** You can often use your credit card to make purchases, which are then delivered directly to your door.

Websites vary enormously in their style and complexity, which can result in some sites needing a more powerful computer in order for you to access them properly. Most information sites will run on any computer you buy.

Beware

There are lots of stories about people stealing bank details from online commerce websites. Make sure you're buying from a reputable source, and that the secure "padlock" icon shows in the browser when you come to enter your payment details.

Meeting People Online

Friends Reunited and Facebook are two social networking sites you may have heard of. Social networking sites are simply websites that have the specific aim of putting people in touch with other people they know, or who have similar interests.

Social networking sites enable you to:

- Display information about yourself, including photos

- Find and interact with people you know, or knew, for example your family, old school friends or ex-colleagues

- Find people with similar interests and join online groups so you can have discussions

Social networking is assumed to be the younger generation's domain because some of the sites have an emphasis on playing games. But there are a number of sites that are particularly popular with seniors:

- Saga Zone is a social networking site designed specifically for the over-50s. You can do everything listed above, safe in the knowledge that you won't be bothered by young people!

Beware

Be careful what information you tell other people about yourself. If possible, be selective about who can view your profile.

Be aware that anything you publish can make it into the public domain so avoid specifics such as exactly where you live or personal details that a criminal might find useful.

19

Internet Phone Calls

Making phone calls over the Internet (also known as voice over IP, VoIP or IP telephony) is something that has only really been possible since broadband (high-speed) Internet connections became the standard for home users.

With a computer you can bypass the normal phone network and turn your Internet connection into a phone line. But before you go ahead and cancel your existing phone line, consider the following:

Advantages

- Most services offer free calls between users using the same network. An example is Skype. Many younger people use Skype to keep up with their family

- You can access your VoIP account anywhere there's a computer with Internet access. So you could call home from holidays abroad for free

- You can usually use the same service for video calls, if you have a web camera. See the next section "Video calling" for more information

- A VoIP account can give you international calls at a drastically reduced cost, or free. These calls are not usually included in your normal phone network tariff

- You aren't restricted to calling people using the same network – it's usually possible to call other numbers for a charge

Disadvantages

- There is often an irritating fraction-of-a-second delay, even with a high-speed Internet connection

- If you're somewhere private and you have a microphone then that's all you need. Otherwise you'll need to invest in either a headset or special phone that plugs into your computer or modem (Internet connection)

Beware

Internet calling isn't necessarily the bargain it appears to be. If your Internet connection is provided by your phone company, then you'll need to pay line rental anyway.

Internet accounts also can't be used to make emergency calls, so you're advised to keep your normal phone line in any case.

Video Calling

If you have a broadband (high-speed) Internet connection then it's easy to see the person you're calling, while you're speaking to them. Armed with only a web cam (a compact digital video camera designed for use over the Internet), your computer becomes a videophone.

Hot tip

There's usually an option to see a small image of what your correspondent is seeing of you, so you can check that you're in the camera view, and that your hair is neat and tidy.

Key advantages of web cams and video calling:

- **A good method of keeping in touch with people far away.** It can make all the difference to see people when you speak to them. Web cams are particularly popular with grandparents who live a long way away or overseas, as it enables them to keep in regular contact with any children (and the children with them) as they grow up

- **Easy to use** – you simply choose the person you want to call from the phone book on your computer, and once they have accepted your call ('picked up the phone') you have access to the picture their camera is taking, and vice versa. (For this reason, the people you're calling need a web cam too)

- **Usually cheap or free.** Although the picture quality is not guaranteed to be excellent, most services, including Skype, don't charge you to video-call other network users of the same service

Digital Photography

A computer enables you to process, edit, store, improve and print digital photos. Together with a decent color printer (which are cheaper to buy than ever before) you won't need to visit a photo lab again.

Managing digital photos on your computer takes a few simple steps:

Beware

If you decide to manage your photos on your computer, then it's important to have a reliable backup plan for your computer. Photos are precious items that it's impossible to replace once they are gone. See Chapter 10 "Getting Set Up" for more information.

1 Connect your camera at any time – unlike traditional cameras you don't have to wait until you've finished the film to see how your photos turned out

2 Copy the photos to your computer. Many cameras come with software that will manage this automatically for you

3 Assign keywords to a photo, to remind you of the key details, and make subsequent searching easy. For example, you could assign the name of a holiday location or occasion, and the people in it

It's also quick and easy to display digital photos on the Internet for friends and family to see, if they have an Internet connection. You can do this using one of a range of free photo sites which enable you to store pictures in electronic "albums". You can choose to protect your photos so that only those you invite can see them, or make them available for anyone to view.

Simpler Household Admin

Many seniors find that a computer can significantly improve their daily lives. You can automate repetitive tasks, like writing and addressing correspondence, save yourself heavy lifting by arranging for online shopping to be delivered to your door, as well as schedule and remind yourself about practical things that need doing throughout the year.

There are some common ways to use a computer to make your home run more smoothly:

- Use online shopping for home delivery. With access to your cupboards while you're doing the list online, you'll always order just what you need

- Create a birthday calendar so you can easily see when all the family birthdays are, and how old people will be. It can even update itself every year!

- Put your address book into a list, and print address labels at Christmas and other holidays

- Write letters, emails and newsletter updates using a word processor

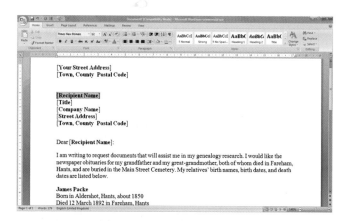

- Manage your bank accounts and pay bills online

- Use a spreadsheet program to do your household budgeting, updating as you go along

Hot tip

There are lots of free web-based tools for helping you organize your life. For example, there are several online to-do list websites, where you can write lists and tick off the items as you achieve them. It gives you a single place to keep all the things you want to do, without losing all those bits of paper...

Creating Family Videos

Having more time for hobbies is one of the biggest benefits of being a senior. If you intend to take up or improve your video skills using family and friends, then a computer will help you to edit the film you take and create movies for display and distribution.

Using software that runs on your computer, it's easy to create professional-looking home videos. You can even create DVDs of your films to send to people.

If you have a digital video camera, it's easy to create family videos to show everyone:

1 Once you've finished filming, connect the camera to the computer using a cable. Check the specific instructions for your camera to ensure that it can connect directly to a computer

2 Transfer the footage to the computer. Most video cameras come with software that will do this automatically – prompting you when you plug it in

3 Use movie-making software to edit your footage and add any features, e.g. soundtrack or messages. You can usually design a menu screen for a DVD version

Beware

Different movie-making software packages vary considerably by ease of use. Read some reviews before you invest a lot of time trying to learn how to use a particular package.

TV and Radio

The Internet is great for finding television and radio programs you may have missed first time round. They are usually on the channel's website, or on fan sites or video sites like YouTube (www.youtube.com).

You can connect a computer to most modern televisions which means you can watch programs you missed from the comfort of your armchair on your big television screen.

To watch catch-up television:

1 **Find the program you are looking for.** Use an Internet search engine or look on the channel's website

2 **Download any software needed.** This will usually happen automatically the first time you try to view a program

3 **Watch or listen at your screen.** Press 'Play' to watch the program on your computer screen, or connect your computer to your television

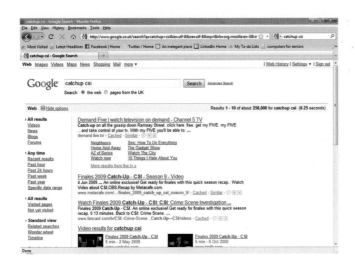

Hot tip

The BBC iPlayer contains all the recently broadcasted material from the BBC. However, it's only available in certain countries, depending on broadcasting rights.

25

Hot tip

It's easy to catch up with radio shows too. Audio downloads, e.g. radio shows or one-off recordings, are often called "podcasts" because they are ideal to listen to on a portable device like an iPod. These can be downloaded instead of listened to online.

Replacing Your VCR

If you are fed up with the picture quality you get on your video recorder, as well as the limited amount of time you can record during a holiday period, then you could consider turning your computer into a recorder of television programs.

You'll need a higher specification computer to do this, because video (images) need a lot of processing power and take up a lot of disk space. You'll also need a TV tuner card.

To turn your computer into a video recorder you need to:

1 Ensure your computer has the additional components you need – a TV tuner card, extra hard drive space and processing power

2 Choose software to use for recording programs. Windows Media Center comes with many PCs as default, or you can choose another similar application

3 Position your computer near to an aerial or cable television supply and plug it in

Listening to Music

With good speakers or headphones you can use a computer to play music CDs and listen to radio stations. You can create and store a jukebox of all your music, and create playlists of your favorite songs.

In addition, a computer can take any music on vinyl or cassette and copy it to CD or turn it into digital files that can be played directly from your computer. This is good for tidying up old records and cassettes – you can move them all to the garage or loft and free up space.

To move your music from vinyl or cassette onto your computer you will need to:

1 Choose a cassette or record deck that will connect to your computer. In most cases you will choose an external unit that plugs in to the computer

2 If you already have a deck, then you can buy a cable to convert the audio cable to a USB cable or "phono in" cable that will plug into your computer's "line in" socket. Make sure you invest in a good quality cable, otherwise the recording sound quality may be affected

3 You'll need software to record the music. Software like Audacity (http://audacity.sourceforge.net) has additional tools like scratch and hiss-reduction filters

4 Once you've copied the music to your computer, you can listen to it, and organize it, using a program like Windows Media Player or iTunes

Hot tip

As well as Windows Media Player, iTunes is another well known music organizer. This works on Macs and PCs and plays videos, music and podcasts. It's free to download from www.apple.com/itunes.

Research Your Hobbies

Regardless of what your interests are, a computer will help you to progress them, which is of course, as seniors, what you should be spending your time on!

Through social networking you can join discussion groups with people of similar interests throughout the world. On the Web you can find more information than you can imagine, on every conceivable topic. That's a lot of information...

Most hobbies are enhanced by use of the Internet. Examples include:

- **Gardening** – learn new methods and solve problems with pests. You can also buy plants and supplies online and have them delivered to your door

- **Genealogy** – research family history and track people through personal and official government websites

- **Photography** – find out about the latest kit, techniques and styles, and display your photos online

- **Arts & Crafts** – join forums of like-minded people; download new patterns and styles, learn new techniques

- **Music** – find out about the latest releases from your favorite artists. Listen to samples before you buy

Beware

Although the Internet is great for finding information, don't forget that many sites are published by enthusiastic amateurs – there is no guarantee that information published is correct.

There have been a number of examples of journalists quoting Wikipedia (an online, publicly updated encyclopaedia) and the facts have been completely wrong!

3 Inside a Computer

Let's face it, the inside of a computer is not very interesting – it's what you'll do with the computer that is important. But in order to get the most from your purchase once it's home, you need to know that you're buying the right equipment.

Computer Essentials

Modern computers are incredibly user-friendly and you need very little, if any, technical knowledge to use or run one. Unlike previous generations of computers, into which you had to type lines of unintelligible instructions, all desktop computers now use a graphic interface.

As a result, you don't really need to know what's inside the computer case, or the technical details of how it works. You can usually rely on the fact that it just does.

But knowing the basics will help you when you're buying your computer. You'll be able to have a sensible conversation about it with a sales assistant, and understand the computer descriptions you see in a shop. It will also help you understand adverts and online descriptions.

This is important because the specification of the computer you buy will affect how it will perform, which in turn will affect the activities that you can achieve with it.

The key steps to successfully investigating and understanding enough to buy a computer are:

Don't forget

A lack of technical understanding is not just an issue for seniors – there are many non-technical people in the younger generations too. The most important thing is to ask, or look things up, when you find that you're missing information.

1 Knowing which key components of a computer are the most important to think about, and which are less important to you

2 Understanding the acronyms and jargon used to describe each component

3 Understanding the basics of how they work

Whether it's a hard drive, memory, processor or other internal component you're looking at, this chapter will take you through all the key components of a computer, and ensure you are knowledgeable about the essentials.

The Inside View

Here's what you get inside a normal desktop computer. These features are fairly standard across most types of computer.

As we describe further in the chapter "Choose Your Type", the features may be smaller or in a different format depending on the type of computer you buy. For example, laptops, netbooks and slimline desktops all have less internal space than a standard desktop machine, so the components are usually smaller and in a different location.

Processor, including cooling fan

Memory

Motherboard

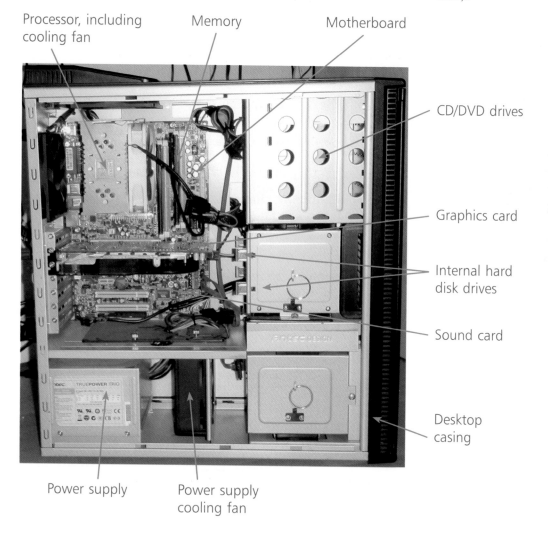

CD/DVD drives

Graphics card

Internal hard disk drives

Sound card

Desktop casing

Power supply

Power supply cooling fan

Processing Power

The processor is the brain of the computer – it's an electronic chip that controls everything else that happens in the computer. It's important to get the right processor because a lack of processing power will restrict some of the activities your computer can handle.

Use the following steps to find the best processor:

1 Look at what's available

2 Choose your speed

3 Get multi-tasking

4 Cache – is it important?

5 Choose your make and model

Beware

If you are interested in buying a Mac computer, you may not have a choice on the processor, as they are often linked to the Mac operating system software that the computer is running. See Chapter 6 "Software" for more information about operating systems.

What's available

Spend some time looking at adverts to see what processors are available for computers in your price range. Although it looks confusing, it's easy to identify the processor when you realize that most names follow a similar pattern (although the name elements aren't always in exactly the same order):

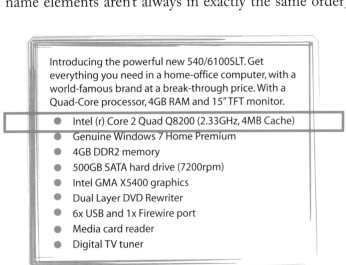

Introducing the powerful new 540/6100SLT. Get everything you need in a home-office computer, with a world-famous brand at a break-through price. With a Quad-Core processor, 4GB RAM and 15" TFT monitor.

- Intel (r) Core 2 Quad Q8200 (2.33GHz, 4MB Cache)
- Genuine Windows 7 Home Premium
- 4GB DDR2 memory
- 500GB SATA hard drive (7200rpm)
- Intel GMA X5400 graphics
- Dual Layer DVD Rewriter
- 6x USB and 1x Firewire port
- Media card reader
- Digital TV tuner

Speed

Processors work very fast, at a speed measured in megahertz (MHz) or gigahertz (GHz). For those of you who know your electronics, physics or Latin, giga is higher than mega, and the higher the number, the faster the processor (and therefore the computer) works. The faster the computer works, the more you can achieve with it.

Multi-tasking

It's now possible to buy a multi-core processor, which is a processor that is able to multi-task – it can process different instructions at the same time in each core. So a dual-core chip generally processes twice as many instructions at once, while a quad core processes up to four times as many instructions at the same time. Obviously the more cores, the faster your computer will work.

Cache

The cache (sometimes called L2 cache) is the waiting room where all the instructions are queued, ready for the processor to receive them for processing. The bigger the cache, the more instructions can be queued and the quicker the processor can work. Cache is usually measured in megabytes (Mb) so again, the higher the number the better.

Make and model

There are two main suppliers of processors – Intel and AMD – and most computers have one of these. In general you are best sticking to these as they are proven to work reliably.

The following are processor ranges that you are likely to come across. Within each range there are a number of different options, with faster processors being more expensive.

- AMD: Athlon, Phenom, Radeon, Semprion, Turion, Opteron

- Intel: Pentium, Celeron, Centrino, Core, Atom

Hot tip

Most processors work so fast that they need a fan to disperse the heat they generate, and most therefore have built-in fans as standard.

The computer also has a fan to keep the power supply cool. So, all in all, you really should keep enough space round the computer for enough air to circulate.

Memory – What's That?

A computer's memory is a bit like the desk in your study. If you have a small desk then you can only spread out a small amount of your work before you run out of room, at which point you have to put that work away before you can start a new task. The bigger the desk, the more you can do without running out of space.

Memory is transient – it's only used to help the computer run while it's turned on. It's not permanent storage. (Just like your desk, which I'm sure you tidy up when you've finished for the day.)

To make sure you get the right memory you need to:

1 Understand the essentials

2 Choose the right amount

3 Plan for the applications you'll be using

4 Future-proofing your memory

Beware

You can decide to add memory at any time in the future. You will need to make sure it's the same type and speed as the original memory. A computer support shop will be able to help you with this.

Introducing the powerful new 540/6100SLT. Get everything you need in a home-office computer, with a world-famous brand at a break-through price. With a Quad-Core processor, 4GB RAM and 15" TFT monitor.

- Intel (r) Core 2 Quad Q8200 (2.33GHz, 4MB Cache)
- Genuine Windows 7 Home Premium
- 4GB DDR2 memory
- 500GB SATA hard drive (7200rpm)
- Intel GMA X5400 graphics
- Dual Layer DVD Rewriter
- 6x USB and 1x Firewire port
- Media card reader
- Digital TV tuner

The essentials

There are a lot of different terms used to describe memory but it's one of the computer areas where you really don't need to worry about it. When you're buying a computer it doesn't matter whether the memory in your computer is called SDRAM, is DDR or DDR2, or what speed it is (usually measured in MHz).

The only really important item is the amount you get, measured in gigabytes (GB). This is a 1GB memory module:

Getting the right amount

In general, the more memory you put in your computer the better it will work. Previous generations of computers required much less memory, measured in megabytes (MB), but this is no longer a viable amount to run a computer – steer clear of any offered with memory in MB.

Applications

Look at any specific software that you are planning to use. If you will be using anything that involves images or movies then you will need more memory. Running simpler text based applications, like email, or web browsing, is less intensive and doesn't require as much memory.

The operating system is one of the most memory-intensive applications you will buy. You may read, or be told, that Windows only needs 1Gb of memory to run. But practical experience has shown that it actually requires a minimum of 2GB, and preferably more if you can afford it.

Beware

A clever feature of Windows enables you to add more memory using a USB key (a small hard drive that you plug in to any free USB slot on your computer). This is a really quick and easy way of making your computer go faster if you find it's too slow.

Future Proofing

Processors

It's not very easy to upgrade a processor once you've bought a computer. It's an integral part of the computer and, as well as having to get the right type and speed, you also have to find one that fits into your particular computer case.

Memory

However, it's possible, and relatively easy, to increase the amount of memory at a later date if you find you don't have enough. In fact, if you find your computer isn't working very well (or seems slow) adding additional memory is usually a cheap fix for the issue.

Your operating system should come with a measuring tool so you can see how much memory is being used at any one time. In the diagram below, the memory is the second dial, and it's at 27% usage, which is fine.

Beware

All computers have a status or "about this computer" window that will tell you how much work your processor and memory is doing. So even if you don't have a whizzy dial like the one shown, you'll still be able to tell if you need more memory.

If you have a skilled member of your family, or a local computer expert or shop nearby, then you can choose to start off with a lower amount of memory and upgrade at a later date if you need to.

If you decide to do this, check the number of memory slots that are currently empty in the machine and therefore available for future expansion.

Without a free space you would have to remove a memory chip from an existing slot and insert a bigger chip instead, which is a waste of good memory!

Introducing Disk Drives

A disk stores data. Unlike the memory, which is cleared when you turn the computer off, the disk is a permanent storage place for all your work and files, including email, word processing documents, spreadsheet files, music, photos and videos.

You can get a number of different types of disk storage:

- **Internal hard disk** – traditional storage found inside the computer (sometimes abbreviated to HDD)

- **External hard disk** – very similar to the internal hard disk but is portable

- **Media drives** – an external hard drive designed specifically for music and other media files

- **Media cards** – small cards designed for use inside smaller devices like cameras, usually used for media files

- **USB key or pen drive** – a small, compact object that can store files

As a general rule, a computer comes with an internal disk drive. External drives and USB keys are sold separately.

CD and DVD drives are also a type of disk drive, and we cover these later in this chapter.

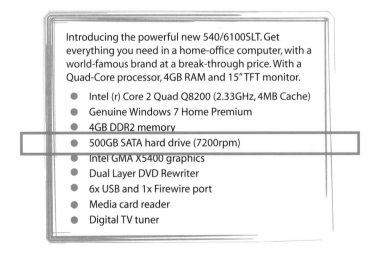

Introducing the powerful new 540/6100SLT. Get everything you need in a home-office computer, with a world-famous brand at a break-through price. With a Quad-Core processor, 4GB RAM and 15" TFT monitor.

- Intel (r) Core 2 Quad Q8200 (2.33GHz, 4MB Cache)
- Genuine Windows 7 Home Premium
- 4GB DDR2 memory
- 500GB SATA hard drive (7200rpm)
- Intel GMA X5400 graphics
- Dual Layer DVD Rewriter
- 6x USB and 1x Firewire port
- Media card reader
- Digital TV tuner

Hot tip

The words disk and drive are often used interchangeably. A hard disk, a hard drive and hard-disk drive are all the same things.

Disk and disc are also interchangeable. Originally "disks" were of magnetic origin and "discs" were optical.

Internal Hard Disk

The hard drive is the standard storage disk that comes in a computer. It's where your files and settings are stored by default. Hard drives are usually simply described by capacity, and sometimes speed.

All computer storage, including internal disk drives are measured in bytes, Megabytes (MB), Gigabytes (GB) and Terabytes (TB).

The key steps in choosing a hard drive are:

 Work out what you'll be using it for

Pictures, movies and videos will take up more space than text documents like Word or Excel. If you have a modern digital camera, each of your photos will take up between 1Mb and 3Mb, so it only takes 1000 of those to get to 1Gb.

 Choosing the right type

The name "SATA" refers to the type of connection used to attach the hard drive to the computer. SATA is the most common and it's good for fast data transfer. Other types include IDE, which has been superseded by SATA.

If you plan to upgrade or change the disk drive then you'll need to get the same type so that it can be fitted in.

 Don't worry about speed

You may see a speed listed against the hard drive which, like a record, shows the number of times that it spins per minute. Although theoretically the faster, the better, it's an area where as a beginner you are unlikely to be able to tell the difference.

Beware

Don't worry about getting the size of your hard drive wrong. It's easy to get extra space at a later date by plugging in an external hard drive. There's no installation required – you simply plug it in and it appears on the screen just like the hard drive that's installed internally.

External Hard Disk

While you should try to buy enough internal storage for all your current and future needs, it's not a disaster if you run out of space in the future. It's very easy to buy additional storage, for example an external hard disk, which simply plugs in and immediately gives you more storage space.

Hot tip

Be careful to check whether the external hard drive you buy needs a power socket. Some smaller drives don't – useful if you have a limited number of free power sockets, or if you're buying a laptop for mobile use.

External hard drives are similar to internal drives but are portable in a protective casing. Depending on the model and size they will probably have their own power supply.

External drives are particularly useful for:

● Overflow – times when you need additional space

● Backups – taking a copy of your files and storing it somewhere separate in case of an unexpected disaster

The main considerations you need to take into account are:

 **1** Capacity

To use an external drive for backup you need to buy one that is bigger than the amount of data you have. Plan for the future – buy something at least the size of the hard drive in your machine.

2 Size and weight

If you plan to carry data around then consider investing in a slightly more expensive, but lighter and more streamlined drive. These vary greatly in size but can be small enough to fit in a handbag or coat pocket.

Media Drive

A media drive is a type of portable external hard drive designed specifically to carry multimedia files. It enables you to quickly and easily take music, photo and video files from your computer and display them on a television.

They are easy to use – you simply copy files from your computer onto the media drive, unplug it and plug it into your television or DVD player.

Consider the following steps to determine if a media drive is right for you:

1 Do you need a specific media drive?

If you are likely to have media files on your computer that you would like to display on your television, for example holiday photos or videos from a family wedding, then a media drive might be a good investment.

2 Choose the features you need

- Remote control – Most media drives come with a remote control, so you can pause, fast forward and rewind anything you are watching, including photos.

- If you have a high-definition (HD) television or home cinema setup in your lounge, then you should choose a media drive that can be set to "upscale" to high definition.

Hot tip

Upscaling is a process that enables a program or files to be displayed in high definition even if they weren't recorded in it. It means you can look at photos or watch films on your high definition television without seeing rough edges.

Media Card Reader

A media card is a small chip-like card that is used inside many smaller devices, for example digital cameras and smartphones. It is used to store media files such as photos, videos, and on smartphones with music players, music too.

Although it's small in physical size, it has a high data capacity – usually a number of gigabytes – which means that it can hold a lot of media files.

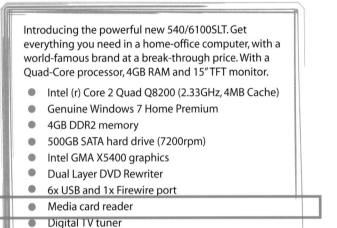

Introducing the powerful new 540/6100SLT. Get everything you need in a home-office computer, with a world-famous brand at a break-through price. With a Quad-Core processor, 4GB RAM and 15" TFT monitor.

- Intel (r) Core 2 Quad Q8200 (2.33GHz, 4MB Cache)
- Genuine Windows 7 Home Premium
- 4GB DDR2 memory
- 500GB SATA hard drive (7200rpm)
- Intel GMA X5400 graphics
- Dual Layer DVD Rewriter
- 6x USB and 1x Firewire port
- Media card reader
- Digital TV tuner

Hot tip

Media cards are the new floppy disk: very few computers come with floppy disk drives these days as they hold so little data compared to these media cards and USB drives.

Many desktop computers now come with a built-in card reader, which enables you to retrieve photos and other media from your mobile devices without having to plug them in. For space reasons laptops don't usually have a built-in card reader, but you can buy them separately – it plugs in using a USB connection.

Introducing CDs and DVDs

CD and DVD drives remain one of the most confusing areas of buying a computer because there are so many format, terms and acronyms that cover both the discs and the drives.

The two main types of disc and disc drive are:

- **CD (compact disc)** – just like your music CDs but used to hold computer files instead of songs

- **DVD (digital versatile disc)** – similar to CDs but able to store many more files

Most desktop computers come with at least one CD or DVD drive as standard (some have two), while smaller computers such as slimline machines, laptops or netbooks may not have a CD drive at all.

You can buy an external CD drive if your computer doesn't have one already. Like external hard drives, they come in a protective casing, and can be used on any machine with a USB connection.

You may find this useful for loading software onto your machine, although this may depend on your Internet connection, as a lot of software can be bought online and downloaded direct to your computer.

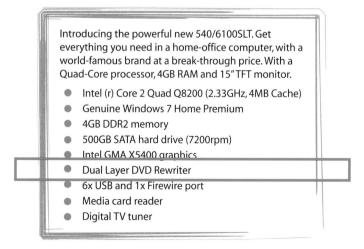

Introducing the powerful new 540/6100SLT. Get everything you need in a home-office computer, with a world-famous brand at a break-through price. With a Quad-Core processor, 4GB RAM and 15" TFT monitor.

- Intel (r) Core 2 Quad Q8200 (2.33GHz, 4MB Cache)
- Genuine Windows 7 Home Premium
- 4GB DDR2 memory
- 500GB SATA hard drive (7200rpm)
- Intel GMA X5400 graphics
- Dual Layer DVD Rewriter
- 6x USB and 1x Firewire port
- Media card reader
- Digital TV tuner

CD and DVD Drives

The obvious use of a CD or DVD drive is to enable you to listen to music CDs or watch films on your computer. In addition, you can use blank discs to store files and data, and load programs or files onto your computer.

A CD and a DVD are made of the same material, and are the same size and shape. A CD format disc can hold approximately 80 minutes of audio or 750MB of data, and a standard DVD format disc can hold approximately 120 minutes of video, or 4.7GB of data.

In order to get the right CD drive you need to:

1 Get the right format drive

If a computer comes with a CD/DVD drive at all, then as standard it will read and write (create) CDs and read DVDs. Many will also write DVDs as standard, which is good for creating backup disks (because a DVD takes more files than a CD) or for creating DVDs of family videos.

Additional options you can choose include:

- Blu-Ray – gives you the ability to play Blu-Ray film discs on your computer.

- Dual layer – the ability to record double the amount of information on a disc. To access this feature you'll need to buy dual layer (DL) discs which are considerably more expensive than standard discs.

2 Consider multiple drives

Most computers will come with a single disc drive. But if you are going to be copying discs, for example family videos, then you should consider investing in a second disc drive. It will save you swapping discs over.

...cont'd

 Speed

Unlike hard disk drives, CD/DVD drives are usually described by how many times faster they go than real time listening. So a 45x drive goes pretty fast, which is good for data copying. Note that the drive won't always go that fast, it usually depends on what activity you're doing.

 Understand the terminology

- Recordable (R) discs can be used to store data on. Although you can delete files off the disc, for example if you copy the wrong file, you cannot re-use the space allowance

- Rewritable (RW) – you can add and remove files without losing any space, until you "finish" it (see below)

- Plus and minus symbols (+ and -). Don't worry about these until you need blank discs – then just make sure you buy a type that works in your drive

- Finishing – until a disc is "finished" it cannot usually be read on other CD or DVD players. It's part of the disc creation process. You can't add more files to a disc once it has been finished

USB Keys

USB keys are amazing little hard drives that come in a variety of shapes, colors and sizes. They have the capacity of a small external hard drive but are highly portable, being only a few centimeters long, and fit neatly into a pocket or handbag.

Advantages

- Highly portable – very small and compact

- Low-cost purchase

- Stores all types of files, including photos, videos and office documents

- Can be written to and deleted from over and over again (unlike CDs/DVDs)

- Easy to install – simply plug it into any free USB slot in the computer

- Useful for copying files to computers without a CD/DVD drive

- Can be set up as a repair disk (used to restart your computer if it breaks)

- Will work as additional memory if your computer is running slowly

Disadvantages

- Not very reliable – sometimes the data corrupts unexpectedly

- Can break easily, particularly the USB slot

- More expensive per gigabyte of space than traditional external hard drives

Beware

Although useful, USB keys have their disadvantages and they should not replace a good sized, reliable external hard drive for permanent storage of large amounts of data.

Sound Cards

In order to be able to play and record sound, a computer needs a sound card, which plugs into one of the sockets inside your computer base unit. (It also needs speakers, which we'll cover later.)

You should do the following:

 Decide if the standard sound card is enough

By default, manufacturers simply insert a basic sound card and this is fine for most people. But if you are doing something that requires particularly good sound quality, for example copying your vinyl collection to CD or MP3, or using your computer as a media center, then you should consider upgrading.

 Choose the right manufacturer

If you're going to the expense of buying a new sound card, consider spending your money on a well known and reliable manufacturer.

The best-known manufacturer is Creative Labs, which produces a range of sound cards called Sound Blaster. Different models provide different features.

 Consider the sound options you want

It's no longer a simple choice between mono and stereo sound. Look at the different options and choose a card that has everything you want.

- Choose 5.1 or 7.1 surround sound if you plan to use your computer for quality music or film watching

- A MIDI socket enables you to connect equipment like an electric keyboard to your computer

- Some cards come with a remote control, enabling you to use your computer like a hi-fi

External devices can be really useful for improving your computer's performance at a later date, so it's less important to get absolutely everything you want up front. However, external devices usually need an electrical socket in order to run, and will require desk or floor space, unlike devices stored in the computer itself.

4 Consider buying a sound card and speakers together

If you don't already have a good quality set of speakers then you may get a more cost-effective deal if you buy a combined speaker/sound card set. This also ensures that you get a similar quality for the two items.

5 Consider upgrading post-purchase instead

If you're not sure if you need to upgrade from the default sound card, you could buy an external sound "card" at a later date. These are easy to install – you simply connect them to your computer using a USB cable.

You could also choose an internal sound card specifically for laptops. This simply pushes into a socket on the side of your laptop and saves using up your USB connections.

Graphics Cards

Also known as a display adapter or video card, a graphics card enables your computer to display and process images.

Similar to sound cards, some computers come with a basic graphics card built into the computer, but you can choose to upgrade to a better-performing model if you want to, or if you are planning to do lots of image-related activies.

There are a number of well known manufacturers of graphics cards, including ATI (now part of AMD), Intel and NVidia.

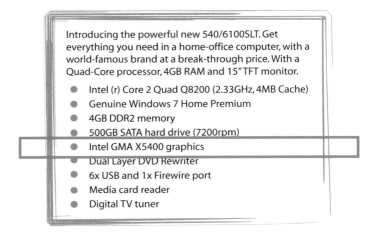

Introducing the powerful new 540/6100SLT. Get everything you need in a home-office computer, with a world-famous brand at a break-through price. With a Quad-Core processor, 4GB RAM and 15" TFT monitor.

- Intel (r) Core 2 Quad Q8200 (2.33GHz, 4MB Cache)
- Genuine Windows 7 Home Premium
- 4GB DDR2 memory
- 500GB SATA hard drive (7200rpm)
- Intel GMA X5400 graphics
- Dual Layer DVD Rewriter
- 6x USB and 1x Firewire port
- Media card reader
- Digital TV tuner

Consider the following steps when choosing a graphics card:

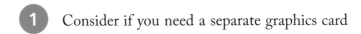 Consider if you need a separate graphics card

In effect, the graphics card contains another processor, which is dedicated to graphics work. So by installing a separate graphics card you help ensure that power-intensive graphics work doesn't divert power from the computer's other processing activities.

So if you want to do any of the following activities on your new computer then you should consider investing in a more powerful graphics card for your computer:

- Home-video editing
- Editing or advanced digital photography or computer art
- Computer programming
- Computer gaming, particularly new, fast or online games
- Using your computer as a VCR

However, for most home users, the graphics capability that comes with the computer will usually be sufficient.

2 Look at specific software packages

If you are planning to buy a specific application, for example digital photo editing software like Photoshop or Photoshop Elements, then check for any minimum requirements listed on the packaging. This will ensure that your software will work perfectly when it's installed on your new machine.

3 Look at how much additional memory comes with the card

Like system memory, graphics card memory is measured in Megabytes (MB) and the more you get, the better graphics display you'll get.

TV Tuner Cards

A TV tuner card enables you to use your computer like a television. As its name conveys, the card contains a tuner, similar to the one in your television. You plug an aerial into the back of your computer and the tuner card receives and displays the programs on your monitor.

Introducing the powerful new 540/6100SLT. Get everything you need in a home-office computer, with a world-famous brand at a break-through price. With a Quad-Core processor, 4GB RAM and 15" TFT monitor.

- Intel (r) Core 2 Quad Q8200 (2.33GHz, 4MB Cache)
- Genuine Windows 7 Home Premium
- 4GB DDR2 memory
- 500GB SATA hard drive (7200rpm)
- Intel GMA X5400 graphics
- Dual Layer DVD Rewriter
- 6x USB and 1x Firewire port
- Media card reader
- Digital TV tuner

Consider these questions to help you buy the right TV tuner card for your computer:

1 Do you need a television tuner at all? Do you want or need television on your computer?

2 Will you be near an aerial socket, and if so, is your aerial digital or analog?

3 Which brand should you look at?

Do you need a TV tuner card?

Watching TV programs in front of your computer will not be as comfortable as sitting in your armchair (unless you're sitting in your armchair with a laptop on your knees!).

Also, the availability of on-demand television services and the number of mainstream digital recording devices (hard disk recorders and PVRs) means that you can already access programs you missed and record transmissions in high quality using your existing television equipment.

Digital versus analog

If you do choose to buy a tuner card, make sure it's a digital card. Digital transmission is taking over in many areas, which renders an analog receiver useless.

Different brands

If you still think you need a TV tuner card, it's worth choosing a well known manufacturer. Although there may not be much difference in picture quality, bigger names tend to spend more money on making their products easier to use and configure. Better to spend the time you have watching the television, not trying to work out how to set it up!

Popular brands you may see include:

- Asus

- Hauppage

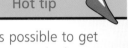

Hot tip

It's possible to get tuner cards that contain both an analog and a digital receiver. This enables you to view, and record, both types of channel on your computer.

51

Upgrading Components

From reading this chapter you should now have a good understanding of what the inside of a computer looks like, which components are important and what you need to know about each component.

This understanding will help you to get the specification computer you need.

Ideally, you would carefully consider the options available before buying a computer that's exactly perfect and will last you for years.

The reality, however, is that any computer you buy may get slower over time because:

- You'll install new software which uses up disk space, memory and other resources

- As you start getting better at using a computer you'll start to use more of the system which, as a result, uses more of these resources

As a result you may need to upgrade your computer later on in its life. Buying something with room to expand will enable you to do this at a lower cost than buying a new computer.

Improving performance

The best machine for expansion is typically a desktop machine, which has a large exterior case with space for a second hard drive or CD/DVD drive. The motherboard also has space for additional graphics and sound cards, if you decide you need something more powerful.

Other machines don't have as much room. A slimline desktop, for example, doesn't usually have room for a second hard disk drive – in this instance you would need to replace the existing drive.

Laptops, by virtue of their compact size, also don't have much expansion space. It's a double whammy – new laptop components are generally more expensive too.

4 Peripherals

In this chapter we look at all the other items you'll need to plug into your computer to make it do the things you want it to.

Introducing Peripherals

For your computer to really be right for you, you'll need to spend some time considering the external components that plug into the computer, known as peripherals. This includes the monitor, input devices like the mouse and keyboard, and output devices like a printer.

Although you may not like to think about it too much, as a senior it is important for you to find computer equipment that is easy to use and doesn't place a strain on your body. For example, some people find a mouse hard to use, either because it's difficult to aim correctly, or because it causes pain in their fingers.

There are lots of assistive computer devices designed specifically for older people, and we'll be looking at some of the options in this chapter.

In addition to choosing these devices well, there are a number of features within software, such as the ability to increase icon and font sizes, and "sticky keys" which we'll cover later on in the book, in the chapter on choosing the right software.

The key steps for ensuring you choose the right external components are:

1 Decide which external devices you are planning to buy

2 Look at the options available and see what the price ranges are

3 Think about which are best from a space and usability point of view

4 Consider senior-friendly alternatives if appropriate

Don't forget

We haven't covered all the peripherals here – there are many more devices available, ranging from the serious to the hilarious. Look out for the mug warmer, and the summer fan, that connect to your computer's USB socket.

Connecting up

Peripherals need to be connected to your computer in order to work. But while some peripherals are always connected to your computer by wires, such as your monitor, others can be connected either by a cable or by wireless.

There are lots of different connection methods with different names, which are usually the technical names of the data transfer method. Often it's up to you to choose which connection you want to use.

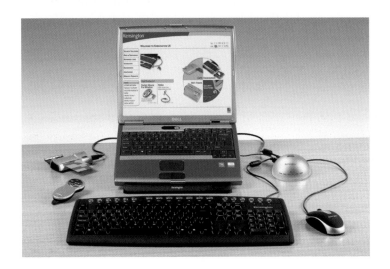

In short, it's just a choice – there's no right or wrong. It usually doesn't matter which connection method you use, wired or wireless.

It's a bit like driving your car from one city to another. There are a number of different roads you could drive along to get to where you're going, and a toll road will generally get you there faster. But you ultimately end up in the same place regardless of the route you take.

It's the same for the data – data travels at different speeds along different routes, and some may be better suited to your needs than others.

Cables and Wireless

USB cables

These days cabling is much simpler – most devices use a standard universal serial bus (USB) cable to connect to a USB port (or socket) on the computer.

There are a number of different sized USB connectors, which are used by different sized devices.

But they are all standard – assuming it's the right size connection, a USB cable will work with any device that supports USB.

Firewire

Also known as I1394, Firewire is another type of wired connection commonly found on computers. Firewire was designed for transferring large amounts of data at high speed and is particularly suited to transferring media files

between devices, for example photos from a camera to your computer, or video from your computer to your media drive.

Computer connections

Connection sockets for these cables are common on computers, both Macs and PCs, so check how many you'll be getting on your new computer. There are usually sockets on the:

● Back of the unit – for devices you don't need to unplug very often, e.g. a mouse or keyboard

● Front of the unit – for easy access to devices that are temporarily plugged in

Some monitors and keyboards also have connection points, which are particularly useful if your computer is a tower unit, under your desk!

Hot tip

Networking appears to be the latest victim of political correctness. The connectors on a networking cable used to be called male and female to distinguish between them – a USB cable now has the imaginatively named "A" and "B" ends.

It's more common now to find peripheral devices that are ready to connect with your computer using a wireless connection. This includes a growing number of printers, scanners and other devices, like digital cameras.

These devices are slightly more expensive than their cabled counterparts, but if you're keen on having a cable-free office or lounge, then they are worth investing in.

Wireless networking is also useful if you want to use a device that is not within a cable length of your computer, or if there are multiple people who want to share the same device.

Wireless

You may already know about Wi-Fi (also known as simply "wireless") without realizing it. This is the same technology which is used for wireless Internet access.

If you have a Wi-Fi-enabled device, then it connects directly to the wireless router (pictured) and becomes part of the network. It's then available for anyone on the network to use, although you can set permissions if you don't want that to be the case.

Bluetooth

Another wireless connection method, Bluetooth was designed to transmit data between devices over a short distance. It's good for sending digital photos from a camera to a computer, or a print request from a computer to a printer.

It doesn't have a very wide field – 10 meters for most devices – plus you need to be in charge of both devices for a connection to be allowed, so it's incredibly secure.

Hot tip

If you see someone in the street wearing an earpiece and talking to themselves, the likelihood is that they are wearing a Bluetooth headset which is wirelessly connected to their mobile phone.

This functionality enables you to hold a conversation using your phone without even taking it out of your pocket or handbag.

Monitors and Displays

If you're buying a desktop computer then the monitor is a component that you'll need to consider. Computer monitors are very similar to modern, high-definition televisions.

For example, a computer monitor is:

- measured by viewable area, in inches from corner to corner, diagonally

- able to take a variety of inputs, e.g. analog, digital or AV connections

- available in a variety of formats, including standard (4:3) and widescreen (16:9)

Most new monitors sold are TFT or LCD flat screens, which means they are:

- only a few inches deep, so they take up considerably less space than the older CRT (traditional style) monitors

- very much lighter, so easier to set up and move around

Laptops and all-in-one computers

If you buy a laptop or all-in-one computer then you'll get an integrated monitor as part of the computer, but the same variations are available. For example, there are widescreen laptops – where the laptop and screen are both wider than usual – and all-in-one PCs come in a variety of screen sizes.

Displays for Seniors

There are a number of key steps to choosing the right monitor for you:

1 Choose a flat screen, for both its lower weight and smaller space requirements

2 Consider spending more money on a larger sized screen – the larger the screen, the more work space. You can see more at once, reducing finger strain from excessive scrolling, and you'll be able to increase font and icon sizes to reduce any strain on your eyes

3 If you have poor eyesight then consider a screen reader or narrator software in conjunction with a large screen. This converts what is displayed on your screen to spoken text

Once you've bought a physical monitor then you'll find that most operating systems have features to make displays easier for older people to use. For example, there are standard desktop themes with larger font sizes and bigger icons.

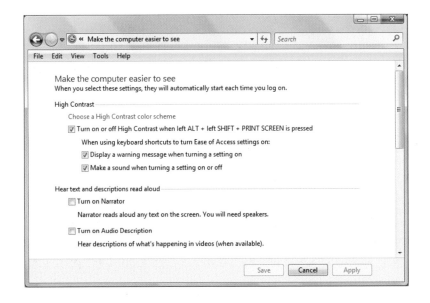

Hot tip

For more information about screen readers, which convert written text to spoken word, read on to the chapter on choosing the right software.

Keyboards

A keyboard enables you to control your computer by typing commands. Although it's a simple device, the keyboard is an important part of your purchase – there are lots of different sizes and styles.

The standard English (UK and US) keyboard is often called a QWERTY keyboard, so called because the letters in the top left read QWERTY. Other countries have keys laid out in different orders, for example France has an AZERTY layout while Germany has QWERTZ!

The standard PC keyboard layout for the UK is shown below. The US keyboard is similar but with some of the symbols in different places.

Beware of these keyboards

Try out keyboards whenever you can, because they vary a lot in design, feel and usability. Some keyboards in particular are not designed with seniors in mind:

● **Compact keyboards**. These are narrower and take up less space but the keys are closer together, which can make it difficult to hit the right keys

● **Keyboards without a number pad**. Often found on laptops, the numbers are superimposed on some of the letter keys towards the right. You access them by pressing a function key in addition to the number, which can be an awkward combination to get right

Keyboards for Seniors

It's a sad fact of life that parts of your body start to let you down as you get older. Keyboards can become particularly hard to use when this happens – poor eyesight and weak fingers are a recipe for frustrating typing errors!

If this is the case for you, consider the following options:

1 A standard keyboard with large print letters printed on the keys makes it easier to see the letters. You can also choose a keyboard with different colored keys so that it's easy to see at-a-glance which key you're pressing

2 A larger keyboard with oversize keys. Similar in concept to a telephone with oversized buttons, you're more likely to hit the correct keys if they are larger and further apart

3 A key guard. This is a plastic keyboard overlay which has holes in so you can press each key. It stops you pressing two keys at once and allows you to rest your hands on the keyboard without pressing keys

For people who have more severe mobility issues, there's a great invention: a one-handed keyboard.

Each letter key has its mirror opposite printed below – so the letter Q is also the letter P, and the letter V is also the letter N – and you access these opposites using a "shift" key.

Although it sounds odd, it enables you to reach all of the letters in the alphabet with one hand, without having to reach across the whole keyboard width.

Hot tip

Another useful feature on a keyboard is shortcut keys. These are usually arranged at the top and enable you to quickly perform the tasks you do the most, for example turning the speaker volume up and down, or opening an Internet browser. On some keyboards they are customizable.

Mouse and Other Devices

A mouse enables you to move a pointer round the screen while pressing the buttons on it (clicking or double-clicking) telling the computer what action you want it to perform.

Most mice have two buttons, left and right, and most have a scroll wheel in the middle, used to quickly move up and down a document or web page.

Some mice have additional buttons on the side or top, and the action performed depends on the mouse, or can be chosen by you.

Many mice sold these days are wireless (the mouse no longer has a tail...) which is good because you aren't restricted by the wire – you can place it anywhere it suits you. But it is another thing that will require occasional battery changes.

If your mouse is wired then it will fit into the standard USB connector, available on all machines.

It sounds so simple, doesn't it! However, the mouse is an item you either love or hate, and as a senior you're more likely to be in the "hate" camp. Like the keyboard, it's a device that can be fiddly to use if your fingers aren't precise, and the pointer can be difficult to see onscreen if your eyesight is poor.

Tracker pads

Some computers, commonly laptops, include a tracker pad, where you use your finger to move the pointer rather than a mouse. They can be difficult to control but some people do prefer them to mice.

Some keyboards also come with a built-in tracker pad. This is particularly useful where you are short on space and don't have room for a mouse as well.

Mouse Alternatives

Most computer systems come with a standard mouse but there are a number of alternatives that you could consider, some of which have been especially designed with seniors in mind.

If you have trouble with mice, consider the following alternative input devices:

1 Would a tracker pad work better for you? With this, you can use your finger to direct the pointer instead of moving the mouse

2 Consider a tracker ball, which is effectively a topsy turvy mouse. The unit stays still and you move the ball, which moves the pointer onscreen. This option reduces the amount of arm movement required

3 Although it may remind you of the computers you saw in the 1980s, a joystick is still a viable alternative to a mouse. Its stick is easy to grasp and move around. There are buttons to replicate the left and right buttons you find on a mouse

Ditch the mouse and keyboard altogether

Alternatively (or additionally) you can reduce your reliance on mice and keyboards by investing in speech recognition software. Using a microphone to speak commands, you can navigate round your computer and its applications, for example dictating documents, letters and emails, and surfing the Internet.

Hot tip

If you find moving devices like mice hard to control, try using keyboard shortcuts instead. For example, pressing Ctrl+P in Microsoft Word brings up the print options, an alternative to using the mouse to click on the File menu, then rolling down to the Print option.

Writing Tablets

Another alternative to mice is a tablet – a square touch-sensitive pad that comes with a pen shaped tool. The first tablets were "graphic tablets" designed for artists and designers to have an easy method of drawing and manipulating images, without having to rely on mice.

But as technology has improved, a tablet now provides a serious alternative to keyboard typing, so if you don't want to learn (or you've found you can't learn new tricks!) then you can write on a tablet in your normal handwriting and your computer will convert it to text or directly into an email. So you can literally write someone an email!

Writing versus graphics tablets

There are two definite groups of tablets: writing and graphics:

- The first is lightweight, simple and, most importantly, cheap to buy, costing roughly the same as a keyboard or mouse

- The second, designed for high end graphic design use, is expensive and is simply not required

The cost of a writing tablet continues to drop all the time, so check current prices and shop around. Simply find one that feels comfortable to use.

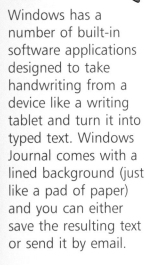

Hot tip

Windows has a number of built-in software applications designed to take handwriting from a device like a writing tablet and turn it into typed text. Windows Journal comes with a lined background (just like a pad of paper) and you can either save the resulting text or send it by email.

Printers

Printing is one of the areas of home computing that has significantly reduced in price while improving in quality. Most home printers are capable of quickly printing good quality color pages and photos.

The main printer used in home computing is the inkjet printer, so called because it mixes jets of ink from different cartridges onto the page, which dries as the page is printed. Inkjets are common because of their combination of quality, reliability and cost.

Common inkjet brands you may consider include:

- Canon

- Hewlett Packard (HP)

- Lexmark

- Brother

- Epson

Ink cartridges

Depending on the printer make and model, your inkjet printer will have either two or four replaceable ink cartridges.

In the two-cartridge machines, one cartridge contains black ink, while the second contains three colored inks: cyan, magenta and yellow. In practice, however, you won't use all three of the colored inks at the same rate, but once one color has run out you'll need to replace the cartridge, even if it means wasting the colored inks that remain.

The answer to this is to choose a printer with four separated ink cartridges. Each color cartridge can be replaced independently as it runs out, which is a much more environmentally and cost-effective solution.

DeskJet printers usually have lights that show you when you need to replace the ink cartridges.

Beware

Before you commit to a printer, check how many pages you'll get per ink cartridge and how much a new cartridge costs. All ink appears expensive but some cartridges last longer than others.

Bizarrely it's often more expensive to buy a set of replacement ink cartridges than it was to buy the printer in the first place!

...cont'd

Other considerations

The right printer for you depends on what you plan to use it for. Consider the following questions to make sure you know what you want from a printer:

1 **What size paper will you be printing on?** Most printers take A4/US Letter paper, but some will do larger sizes

2 **How fast does it print a page (black/white and color)?** This is not a vital point but can be a deciding factor if one printer is significantly quicker

3 **Does it print good quality images?** Measured in dots per inch (dpi), and the higher the figure, the better resolution your images will be

4 **How much space does the printer need?** Look carefully at all the flaps and holes and work out where the paper goes in and comes out. This gives you a true indication of the space required

5 **Where will you locate your printer?** Some printers contain a wireless connection which gives you more freedom about where you can locate the printer

6 **Will you be using your printer "on the move"?** A smaller printer can be taken on holiday to print picture postcards. Or to a meeting to print name badges. Consider what you'll be using your printer for

Hot tip

Another possible printer is the Laser. Traditionally office printers, there are now cheaper models designed for home use. They are still more expensive than inkjets and take up a lot of space but produce a good quality print.

Photo Printers

If you want to print high quality photos then you should consider investing in an additional photo printer.

While a good inkjet printer will produce a passable photo (using specific photo ink cartridges and photographic paper) a dye sublimation (dye sub) printer can produce photo quality prints, on photo paper.

A dye sub printer uses a ribbon instead of liquid ink, and the photo paper passes through the printer four times: once to apply each of the three colors and one final time to apply a transparent coating. It's a slower printing option.

Most dye sub printers are designed to print 6x4 photos and are compact and portable as a result.

Hot tip

If you have the right digital camera and a photo printer then you may not need a computer at all. You simply connect your camera, choose the picture to print, check it on the printer screen and out it comes!

However, there are lots of other things to do on a computer, so do read on!

67

Think about the costs

If time is not of the essence in your photo printing, then work out the true cost of photo printing before you invest in a specialist printer.

Taking into account the cost of photographic paper and ink, the most cost-effective way to get decent digital photos is often still to take your disc or memory card to a shop. An added bonus is having prints on proper photo paper.

Alternatively there are a number of photo development websites where you can upload your photos, which they print and post back a week later.

Scanners

A scanner is a device that creates a two-dimensional electronic image of a document or object.

The resulting image is a standard computer file that can be stored and treated like any other image, and used as required. For example, you can print, edit or email the scanned file.

Using optical character recognition (OCR) software, you can scan a written document (typed, or in some cases handwritten) and convert it into an editable text file, a document that can be opened using word processing software.

You can use a scanner to:

- Turn printed photos or negatives into digital photos which can be tagged, stored and turned into slide shows. You can also improve old photos, for example brightening any colors that have faded

- Create an electronic file from a paper document so that it can be used electronically. For example, scanning recipes so that you can store and tag them, enabling you to search them by ingredients

- Extracting the text from a document that only exists in paper format so that you don't have to retype it

The most common and cost effective scanner for home use is a flatbed. This is suitable for scanning individual flat and non-flat objects.

If you want to scan a large number of photo negatives then consider a negative scanner – designed specially for photographic negatives and used by photographers. It is more expensive than other scanners but is a less hassle-some way to produce good quality images from negatives.

All-in-one Units

If you are planning to buy a printer and a scanner then why not consider an all-in-one scanner, copier and printer?

An all-in-one provides the same quality scanning and printing as an individual machine, but it takes up considerably less space.

To use the all-in-one as a printer, you simply connect the unit to your computer as you would a printer, either using a USB connection, or wirelessly. For scanning and copying, simply press the appropriate buttons on the unit – you don't even need your computer turned on for copying.

Additional options

- Wireless – You'll generally pay more for a wireless unit, but this gives you greater flexibility about where you put the unit. It also enables multiple computers to use the unit without needing a switch or sharing device

- Card reader. Choosing an all-in-one with a card reader enables you to print images directly from a digital camera storage card without needing to use the computer

Speakers

Most people will want to have decent speakers attached to their computer. This enables you to listen to music and hear sounds, whether it's on videos, websites or while you're using a web cam.

In addition, speakers will enable you to use some of the senior-friendly computer features, for example narration (where the text onscreen is read out to you).

Choosing speakers

The variety of available products has increased in line with the greater use of computers as a media center. Computer speakers now rival in quality those that come with a respectable hi-fi or CD player.

In fact, many of the traditional audio manufacturers, like Sony, Phillips, Panasonic and Samsung, now make computer speakers. Other companies like Logitech and Altec Lansing have developed speakers specifically for computers and digital devices.

You will usually get basic speakers as standard with any computer you buy, consisting of two speakers providing stereo sound. Your sound card may come with additional features such as a sound equalizer, but this is unlikely to have a significant effect on the sound produced.

The speakers connect into the computer using a standard jack plug. In addition, you'll usually need a free power socket.

Hot tip

Many computers, particularly laptops, come with built-in speakers. So check whether the sound quality is good enough before you invest money in another set.

Additional options

For most people, the standard speaker set provided by your computer retailer will suffice. However, consider the following scenarios:

1 Will you be using your computer as a media center, i.e. to watch television, films or videos?

2 Will you regularly listen to music on your computer?

3 Do you plan to turn your old tapes or records into CDs or digital files?

If you answered "Yes" to any of these questions then you should consider upgrading to something with more features.

You can buy speakers with the following options:

- Surround sound – choose from 5.1 or 7.1 depending on the model

- Headphones and microphone sockets

- Remote control

- Karaoke option – a function where the melody line in a song is suppressed so you can plug in a microphone and sing along!

Hot tip

If you are planning to use your computer to watch or record television, then plug the base unit directly into the television. This reduces the number of sets of speakers you'll need to have.

Web Cams

A web cam is a digital video camera designed for use on the Internet and usually used for video calling. Some people also use one to create videos of themselves to send to people.

You can get online with a basic, low quality web cam at a cost of only a few pounds or dollars. However, spending more will give you a better picture quality, a built-in microphone or other features. Top end web cams even include automatic tracking – the web cam follows you as you move around, so that you're always in view.

Hot tip

Web cams can be used to take still photos too. So if you need a digital photo to upload, for example as a profile picture, then you can do that using your web cam.

Consider the following when looking at web cams:

- **Resolution**. Starts at 640 x 480 pixels, which gives you a clear picture only at very small sizes, so choose a web cam that shows pictures in megapixels, the higher the better

- **Frames per second (FPS)**. The more FPS the better the experience – a minimum of 30 FPS for video calling

- **Microphone**. Not included on all models but necessary for video calling if you want to speak to the other party

Nearly all web cams will enable you to take still photos in addition to video.

Options you can choose from on more expensive models include a zoom, automatic tracking and remote controls.

5 Choose Your Type

Do you have a study, or just a lounge? Do you want funky or discreet? Will you be taking your beloved new computer on holiday with you? You'll need to pick the right type for your needs.

Choosing a Computer

Computers come in all shapes, sizes and colors, so whether you're looking for something for your home office, or a more portable device, there's something for everyone.

The right computer for you depends on a number of different lifestyle factors: for example, what you will be using it for; the space you have available; and whether you want to be able to work on the move.

Beware

There's quite a difference in price between the different models. We'll cover this in more detail but, for example, you'll pay significantly more for the same specification machine if it's a laptop or all-in-one computer.

In this chapter we'll look at the different types of computer currently available. The key steps to choosing are:

1 Think about how you'll be using your computer

2 Decide whether a Mac or Windows PC best matches what you're looking for

3 Choose the model that best suits your needs, e.g. a desktop, portable or all-in-one

4 Look at the costs of the different options

Using Your Computer

To help you decide which type of computer is right for you, think about the following questions as you read the information in this chapter:

- Will you usually be at home when you use your computer?

- Or do you travel a lot? Would you like to take your computer with you?

- Do you have a dedicated office, or will you be using the dining room table?

- Would you prefer your computer to be hidden from view when it's not in use?

- How much space is there where your computer will be located?

- Are you particularly keen to have a stylish looking computer? Are you prepared to pay more for style?

- Would you be prepared to spend extra money for additional functionality?

- Or would you prefer a value model?

- Do you have a mobile phone or other device that you want to connect to your computer?

Don't forget

Not all computers are gray and box-shaped these days. There are lots of computers of all shapes, sizes and colors. Some even have designer-inspired colors and patterns. It's OK to choose a computer for its look, but don't forget it has to perform too!

PCs versus Macs

You may already have heard the two abbreviations: PC (for Personal Computer) and Mac (for Macintosh), both of which are types of home computer that have been around since the 1980s. The PC was invented by Xerox and popularized by Bill Gates when he invented Microsoft Windows, while the Mac was invented by Apple. In fact, it was the Mac that first had the desktop with icons – it came to Windows much later.

Comparing the two types of machine is a bit like comparing two very different houses: while they are both made from the same building blocks and enable you to perform the same tasks (e.g. sleep in a bedroom; cook in a kitchen) each one has its own style and, as a result, cost.

PCs

PCs are made from standard components, manufactured by a wide range of companies. Therefore you'll see lots of different manufacturers around: Compaq, Hewlett Packard, Asus, Dell, etc.

There are lots of manufacturers for internal PC components too, so it's easy to find cheap replacement parts if anything breaks or you want to upgrade, or improve, a particular feature.

The main operating system – the piece of master software that runs the computer – for PCs is Windows, produced by Microsoft. You may see different versions of Windows depending on what PC you're using, e.g. Windows 7, Windows Vista, Windows CE.

76

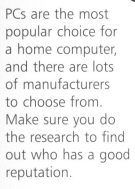

Hot tip

PCs are the most popular choice for a home computer, and there are lots of manufacturers to choose from. Make sure you do the research to find out who has a good reputation.

Some PCs run Linux instead of Windows. Although Linux is becoming more common, it is not as well supported as Windows, both in terms of the number of shops that support it, and in the amount of mainstream software that is available.

Macs

Unlike PCs which are manufactured by a number of different manufacturers, the Mac computer is made and sold by one company – Apple.

As a result, Macs are more expensive to buy than PCs, because there isn't such a large supply of different component manufacturers. However, because Apple is more in control of  its manufacturing process, there are less issues with compatibility, and this means that Macs are less likely to suffer hardware conflicts.

The operating system for Macs is called Mac OS (Mac Operating System), which again, is created by Apple and only available for use on Apple Macs.

Other reasons Mac users give for why you should buy a Mac instead of a PC:

- Mac software is more intuitive, quicker to learn and easier to use than its Windows equivalents

- A Mac needs less configuration. It "just works"

- Macs are less likely to get viruses (although it is still advisable to get anti-virus software, just in case)

- Macs are better able to cope with multimedia without having to get specialist hardware or software

Hot tip

Roughly one tenth of home computers currently sold are Macs, but most Mac owners are great fans and say that they would never again consider buying a PC. Many Mac owners claim that although it's a more expensive initial cost, the lifetime cost of a Mac is less than a PC as they break far less often!

Desktops

The term "desktop" is a hangover from the origin of personal computers. The desktop PC was noteworthy because it made computers accessible to individuals and home users. Up to that point, computers had been large, room-sized mainframe machines found in large companies.

These days, the term "desktop" describes a computer system where the main unit, screen, keyboard and mouse are all separate units.

Beware

"Desktop" is really a misnomer, because it's now as common to find computers where the main unit is a "tower" – a computer case designed to stand up, which can be located as equally on the floor as on top of your desk.

Space requirements

Desktops take up the most space and are only suitable for locations where they can remain set up. The main unit and monitor can be heavy and you shouldn't risk straining yourself by moving these around unnecessarily.

A desktop computer therefore particularly suits a separate office, study, spare room, or study corner if you don't have an extra room.

You should consider a portable machine, e.g. a laptop if you only have the dining room table.

You should also think about power requirements. With a desktop computer the screen and base unit both require power, as will any speakers and other peripherals you choose.

Why Buy a Desktop

A desktop computer offers a good combination of price and features, and will be the best option for many people.

Value for money

- Desktops are generally the most cost-effective option because you get the most for your money. Spend the same amount on a laptop and you'll get a considerably less powerful machine

- Replacement parts are cheaper than for smaller computers, so if something breaks it's always viable to replace the parts

Future-proofing

- Because it's physically a big unit, a desktop usually has plenty of spare space inside which can be used for upgrading – adding new parts as they are needed – so you can go for longer without having to buy a new computer

- This means you can keep the computer you buy for as long as possible, without having to invest time and effort buying and learning how to use a new machine

Usability

As an older person, it's important that the computer you buy is easy to use without causing you discomfort. A desktop computer is ideal for this:

- All the different parts – screen, keyboard, mouse, etc – can be individually placed on a desk and moved to the optimal position for comfortable sitting. This is not possible with a laptop, for example

- There is a full-size keyboard, and plenty of mouse-like tracker balls designed for older people, so you won't strain your fingers

- It's easy to choose or upgrade individual elements to suit your needs, for example buying a larger screen – useful for people with bad eyesight

Don't forget

A desktop machine is a good combination of features and value for money.

It's easy to move components around on a desk until you've found the optimum positions for you.

Slimline Desktops

Slimline desktops are smaller and more compact than traditional desktops, which means they take up less desk or table space.

You can choose between a slimline tower computer and one of the more modern, artistic and funky units that manufacturers have had fun designing and producing.

Advantages of a slimline computer:

- The best of both worlds – a computer that uses standard components, readily available and relatively cheap, in a box that takes up less room than a standard desktop

- If you're planning to use your computer as a media center, then a slimline option will look more like a traditional media unit, and take up less space than a standard desktop

Disadvantages of a slimline computer:

- They usually cost slightly more than their full-size equivalents

- There is less internal space, which means you get fewer features and less future upgrade possibilities

All-in-one Computers

"All-in-one" is a slightly confusing name for a computer as, although the screen and main unit are usually combined, the keyboard and mouse are usually separate. Apple was the first to do this with the iMac – the best-selling Apple computer of all time.

Modern all-in-one computers are usually sleek, combining the processor unit into a remarkably thin screen unit. However, this is usually achieved by using smaller and more expensive laptop-style components, so an all-in-one computer is more expensive to purchase and maintain.

Beware

Don't be confused into thinking that an all-in-one is portable. It's still a desktop machine, designed to be set up and used in a semi-permanent location.

Advantages of an all-in-one computer:

- It takes up considerably less space, has fewer trailing wires and requires fewer power sockets

- It's easy to set up – you simply plug in the power lead and keyboard, and it's ready to use

Disadvantages of an all-in-one computer:

- They cost more than both a standard and slimline unit, because of the technology involved in creating the unit

- The unit design makes it very difficult to fix or investigate problems yourself

Laptops

Not all laptops are created equal – they vary considerably in size, weight and cost, so think about what you'll be using it for before you buy it. Common laptops varieties include:

- **Home use (or desktop replacement).** Generally has a bigger screen and more powerful components than a standard laptop. As a result, it's usually bigger, heavier and often has a shorter battery life

- **Standard.** A typical laptop that is portable. Different models vary a lot in weight

- **Ultra-portable.** A very thin and light laptop, usually with fewer features and a smaller screen. These often don't have built-in CD drives so take up less space

Beware

It's great to have the idea of a desk you can clean at the end of the day, by closing and putting away the laptop. But don't forget you're also likely to have other units, for example a printer. Consider where you'll store those additional devices too.

Space requirements

A laptop is clearly smaller and requires less space than a desktop machine, which makes it a good choice if you don't have a permanent location in mind for your computer work.

You will have significantly fewer wires with a laptop – a single power lead for the unit which means you don't need as many power sockets available.

A laptop's size also makes it easy to store – it's quite feasible to pack your laptop into a cupboard or drawer at the end of the day, or in anticipation of having children to visit.

You do need to be careful about where you store your laptop as they are easy to damage if dropped or heavily banged. You should invest in a padded case.

Why Buy a Laptop

A laptop is a good option for buyers who want the advantages of a portable machine but you do have to pay slightly more as well as losing some of the usability of a desktop machine.

Value for money

- You don't get as much for your money as you would get if you bought a desktop machine, as it costs more to make the smaller laptop components

- You'll probably need to invest in items that would be included in the cost of a desktop, e.g. an external mouse

Future-proofing

- It's harder to upgrade a laptop as there's no internal space, for example to add more memory or additional hard drives. You have to replace what's already there, which a) is more expensive, and b) a more complex job

- Laptops can wear out quicker than desktops, for several reasons: they produce more heat, which affects the internal components, and they are more susceptible to damage as they are moved around

Usability

Older people don't generally find laptops as easy to use as desktop machines.

- The keys are often closer together, and some even have smaller keys, so it's harder to use and can result in strain on your fingers or wrist

- Because everything is in a single unit you can't reposition the individual items to make it a more comfortable experience

Although laptops are in general less comfortable to use than desktops, they are still the right choice if you don't have the space or you do want to travel with your computer. And there are some great laptops available.

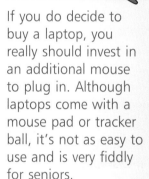

Hot tip

If you do decide to buy a laptop, you really should invest in an additional mouse to plug in. Although laptops come with a mouse pad or tracker ball, it's not as easy to use and is very fiddly for seniors.

Netbooks

Netbooks are very small, lightweight laptops optmized for Internet, email and word processing use. They range in price from fairly expensive – overlapping with low-end laptops – to amazingly cheap.

The more expensive netbooks are really low-specification laptops, manufactured by companies that already make laptops. They run Windows and well known applications like Microsoft Word, Excel and Internet Explorer.

At the cheaper end of the spectrum, there are an increasing number of little-known manufacturers who provide a basic own-brand netbook. These often run the Linux operating system and contain Linux equivalents of Windows or Mac applications.

For these cheap computers, the reduction in cost is achieved by removing expensive parts like the optical CD/DVD drive, and by using different components inside. As a result, these cheap netbooks are usually not upgradeable.

Beware

Beware netbooks with tiny keyboards. Not only are the keys themselves really small, the keys have often been moved around from their usual locations.

Space requirements

Netbooks are the ultimate in space-saving appliances. With the smaller units measuring as little as 20cm by 15cm, you really don't need much space to use one.

Why Buy a Netbook

A netbook is a viable option for anyone who has basic requirements, mostly accessing the Internet and emails. However, many netbooks are bought as a cheap secondary computer, either to provide computer access for two users simultaneously, or for use on the move.

Value for money

- Buying a netbook is definitely the cheapest way to get a computer: on average a netbook costs half to two-thirds of the price of a laptop or desktop

- However, if the netbook will be your only computer, consider whether paying more and upgrading to a bottom-of-the-range laptop (which opens up access to more applications and features) would better suit your needs

- The battery life of a netbook can be as little as three hours, so you may want to invest in a bigger or additional battery

Future-proofing

- Most cheap netbooks are difficult or impossible to upgrade, so once it becomes obsolete, for example you run out of hard disk space, you'll need to invest in an entirely new machine

- Likewise, if the netbook breaks, you'll have to buy a new unit. Check the warranty and service options available

Usability

If you choose a netbook then you'll have all the same potential usability issues as with a laptop. In some cases the issues are even more pronounced:

- The screen is likely to be very small, and there will not be the same range of options to make it easier to read

- The keyboard will be very small and you may find it difficult to type without accidentally touching the surrounding letters

Beware

The starting point for a netbook is that it is low in features. For some models you can choose to upgrade some features at order point. But beware of how quickly the costs mount up. At some point you will be better off buying a laptop that initially appears more expensive.

Mobile Considerations

The overwhelming advantage to a laptop or netbook is that it's portable – you can take it with you wherever you go. You can take it out and about, to keep in touch with friends and family, or while you're on holiday.

Looking after your laptop

If you intend to really make the most of your portable computer, here are a few things you should think about:

- Don't leave it in the car or on display – laptops and phones are quick and easy to pick up and remove and in many cases won't be covered by insurance

- Check if it needs adding to your household insurance policy

- Use a Kensington lock to attach it to a desk. You can take this with you on holiday

- Invest in a carry case that's comfortable to use and will protect your computer from knocks

- It's best not to use the laptop on your lap. It's really not good posture

- Don't forget that if you're going abroad that you will need a plug adapter for it

- Consider investing in a spare battery if you are likely to be away from charging points for any considerable amount of time

6 Software

Software is a really important part of your computer purchase. Choosing the right software enables you to really make the most of your computer. Importantly, you don't always need to spend a lot of money to get good software.

Choosing Software

You should think about what software you will need before you buy your computer so that you can:

● Ensure that you buy a machine able to run any particular software packages you want to use

● Take into account the cost of any software you want

It's easy to underestimate the cost of software – for example, buying the Microsoft Office suite of programs can add 20% onto the cost of a cheap laptop.

Some software has minimum hardware requirements – which means that it needs a certain processor or a minimum amount of memory in order to work properly. You'll need to take this into account when choosing a model of computer, otherwise you'll find that the software won't work properly.

Free software

In the last few years there has been a move towards sharing software – it's much easier to get good software for free:

● Each new generation of PCs and Macs comes with a wider range of integrated software packages, in an effort to convince you to buy it

● There has been significant growth in the number of people developing software for anyone to use for free (freeware) or for a small donation (shareware)

● The Open Source movement has become more mainstream. Open Source software is usually created by a number of software developers collaborating, sometimes countries apart. The result is professional software, regularly updated, for anyone to use for little or no charge

Hot tip

You can get a lot of software for free, especially if you're prepared to put up with the display of adverts. Even if you have a specific requirement, chances are that someone has already created something that will achieve it.

Use a software download site like download.cnet.com to find the type of application you're looking for.

...cont'd

There are a number of different ways to get software:

- **Pre-installed on your machine.** Some programs will already be installed on your machine when you receive it. You may need to fill in some details the first time you use it, but otherwise it's ready to use.

- **On disc, bought from a shop.** Software traditionally comes on a CD or DVD in a large cardboard box. You can buy it from a large number of shops, including larger bookshops.

- **Downloaded from the Internet.** You can buy software from online Internet stores and download it immediately. This is great for getting software immediately, but it can take a long time to download, and significantly impact your Internet data download quota if you have one.

  Additionally, you won't receive discs if you download software from the Internet. So you'll have to download it again if anything goes wrong with the installation.

As a trial
Some software is available as a free trial. You'll usually have a number of days to try it before you have to buy a licence in order to continue using it.

Beware

It's illegal to use software on more than one machine, unless its licence allows it. In fact, modern software often uses an online database to track licence codes, which will even prevent you from installing it on another machine.

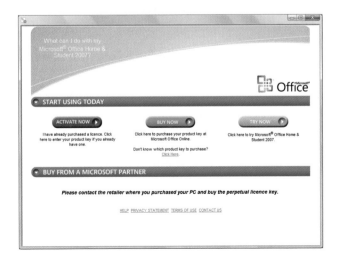

Operating Systems

The operating system is the complex program that enables all the different parts of your computer to work together. It talks to all the internal and external components, and registers input from your keyboard and mouse, so that the computer does what you want it to.

By default, the operating system enables all the basic parts of the computer to work, e.g. the mouse, the keyboard, monitor or display etc. But if you have anything other than a generic item, e.g. you have an unusual size of monitor or a tracker ball instead of a mouse, then you'll need to install additional "drivers" for these – specific software created by the manufacturer to cater for these functions.

These drivers are free, and are usually installed on the machine when it arrives. If not, or you need them again at a later date, the driver software is available on the website of the manufacturer. You'll be given instructions to follow if required.

The operating system and drivers will all be installed on the computer when it arrives.

There are three main operating systems available:

Windows
The most common operating system, currently installed on approximately 90% of desktop machines.

Mac OS
Developed by Apple specifically for Mac computers. Mac OS isn't available on other makes of computer.

Linux
An open-source system that looks similar to both Windows and Mac OS. It's common on netbooks because it doesn't take up much disk space or use many system resources, but you're unlikely to find it on an average desktop computer, or standard laptop.

Don't forget

Choose an operating system for the applications it runs, not just because of its name. Although Windows is more common, you may find that more applications you want to own run under Mac OS.

Microsoft Windows

Windows is the most common operating system for personal computers and is installed on approximately 90% of the units sold throughout the world.

The first version of Windows was launched in 1985 in response to the increasing interest in the Mac graphical interface. The Windows software developed over time, becoming easier to use, with more features.

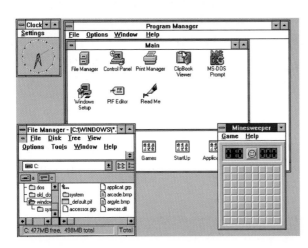

Beware

The latest version of Windows is Windows 7, and the previous version was Windows Vista. Beware anyone selling you a computer with Vista.

There have been a number of different incarnations of Windows since then, with two key turning points:

- The introduction of Windows 95, in 1995, brought in the Start menu and taskbar to make Windows much more user-friendly and rival the Mac. These features have been a common theme in Windows releases since

- Windows XP, released in 2001, kept the same look and feel but was completely redesigned under the hood, resulting in a better, more stable program

There have been many versions of Windows in between, but the current version of Windows – Windows 7 – still has the same design elements, although it has many more advanced features, for example better search functionality and enhanced security.

...cont'd

Key points about Windows

Because Windows is the most common operating system:

- It's the operating system that most technical people know about, so it's easier to find help

- There is a larger number of software applications available for Windows than any other operating system

- There are larger numbers of Windows users in forums on the Internet, so you can usually find someone with experience of doing what you want to

The Windows desktop

Desktop area – can hold files and shortcuts

Widgets – mini applications that give you quick access to the information and tools you need

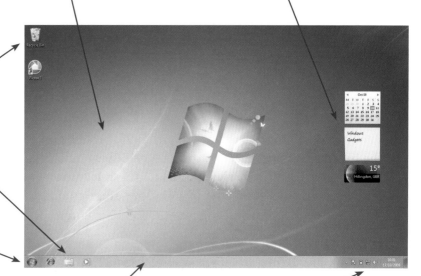

Recycle bin – where deleted files go

Quick launch icons – shortcuts

Start button – the hub of your access to the computer

Task bar – displays all the open windows. Hover the mouse over the name to see a picture of each one

System tray – displays the current status of services running on your computer

Mac OS

Mac OS is the operating system that comes on all Apple Mac computers – both desktops and laptops. It is only available for Macs, so you have to buy one to get it.

Mac OS is currently used by fewer than 10% of personal computer users, but they're a fanatical and vocal minority! Their experience is that Macs and Mac OS are significantly more user-friendly and reliable than their equivalent Windows PCs.

Macs first appeared in 1984 and were the first personal computers to use a graphical interface to manage the computer, instead of text commands. This made it an instant hit with home users and it became increasingly popular.

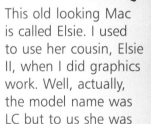

Hot tip

This old looking Mac is called Elsie. I used to use her cousin, Elsie II, when I did graphics work. Well, actually, the model name was LC but to us she was always Elsie.

By the 1990s, however, the Mac was completely overtaken in popularity and sales by Windows and PCs, and Macs became known as the "designer's choice", because its main audience was designers using the graphical design software that was most commonly available on the Mac.

Apple and Macs have seen a resurgence over the last few years, linked in part to the popularity of the iPod digital music player and the iPhone web-enabled mobile phone. As these items become more popular among consumers, more people are seriously considering a Mac computer as an alternative to Windows.

...cont'd

Key points about Mac OS

In 1999, Apple brought out a new type of operating system: Mac OS X, which they've continued to build on.

- Mac OS X is secure and reliable, as it's heavily based on Unix, a secure and reliable operating system

- Macs rarely crash, as this is usually caused by hardware/ software compatibility issues, but Apple makes both parts, reducing the issues

- Macs very rarely get viruses (although this may be because they are less popular machines)

The Mac desktop

System tray – displays the current status of services running on your computer

Macintosh HD– displays the contents of your computer

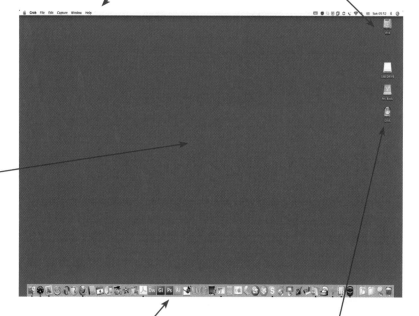

Desktop area – can hold files and shortcuts

The Dock – a combination of the Windows task bar and quick launch icons

Recycle bin – where deleted files go

Linux

Until recently the Linux operating system was more commonly found on servers, but it is now being used on a number of personal computers, though usually only on low end netbooks and some smartphones (see Chapter 11, Going Mobile for more information).

Requiring low processing power and little disk space, Linux is particularly suitable for smaller and less powerful devices, such as netbooks and some smartphones (mobile phones on which you can send and receive email and browse websites).

The Linux operating system was developed in the 1990s and is based on Unix. It's secure and reliable and has a windows-style look and feel, with a desktop, icons and menus.

Key points about Linux

● Although Linux is used on many portable devices, it's not as widely used on desktop machines, so there is less support available for non-expert users

● It's more difficult to find software. Unlike Mac and Windows software, you are less likely to find Linux applications in the shops

The Linux desktop

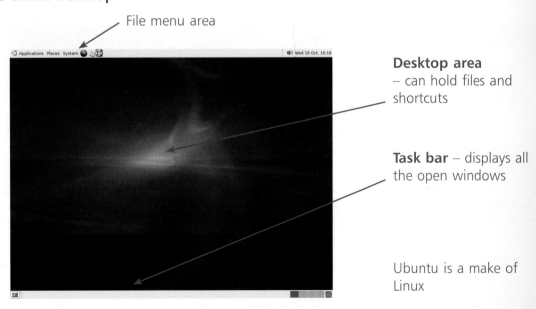

File menu area

Desktop area – can hold files and shortcuts

Task bar – displays all the open windows

Ubuntu is a make of Linux

Preventing Viruses

Viruses and other malware (an abbreviation of malicious software) are common on computers. They are bits of software that spread from computer to computer, usually through emails or Internet downloads. As a result, anti-virus and Internet security software is a necessity.

The first viruses that appeared, in the 80s, were written as an intellectual exercise by computer geeks. However, many of the malware and viruses in circulation today are produced with a commercial or fraudulent aim. For example:

- Some malware programs redirect search engine results to fake results pages – where the person who created the page makes money on every link clicked

- Some go one stage further and "watch" your machine, so they can take away the information you type in, such as passwords and personal details

Good anti-virus software checks your Internet traffic and email (incoming and outgoing) for signs of viruses and malware, as well as performing a full virus scan of your computer on a regular basis. It also has regular, automatic updates, as new viruses are being developed all the time.

Security Center
– this program shows you how well your computer is protected and if any part of your security needs attention.

McAfee SecurityCenter

...cont'd

What comes as standard?

Neither Macs nor Windows PCs come with a built-in anti-virus package but there is a wide range of security software programs you can buy, as well as some free packages.

Getting the software you need

1 For Windows PCs look at the well known makes, including McAfee, Norton (previously Symantec) and Kaspersky. There is generally very little to choose between them – look for special offers

2 For Macs, decide if you are going to buy anti-virus (recommended). If you do, then look at McAfee for the Mac, Norton and Intego VirusBarrier

3 Sign-up to a regular update program. This will automatically download new virus information every day, so you're always completely protected

Cheaper alternatives you could consider

Some companies produce free anti-virus checkers. This is a bona fide option – the companies usually do it to promote their "paid-for" version, which contains more features and is better supported.

- **Windows** – Trend, Panda and AVG Free

- **Mac** – iAntiVirus and ClamXAV (highly recommended)

An alternative is to buy a complete Internet security suite, which saves money on buying individual packages. It also provides your computer with protection in addition to anti-virus.

See the next section for more information about preventing attacks.

Beware

Check carefully to see if you have anti-virus software pre-installed on your computer, either as a full version or as a time-limited trial.

Anti-virus software tends to interact badly with other anti-virus software so, if possible, go with anything that's already installed.

Preventing Attacks

A risk of connecting to the Internet is that people or automated programs may try to connect, or "hack in" to your computer. There is usually a commercial aim to hacking, for example to install malware that tracks the keys you press when typing passwords, before then sending the details out to people who will try to access your accounts.

A firewall manages the connections between your computer and the Internet. As well as stopping unwanted connections reaching your computer from the Internet, it also watches outgoing connections, in case a piece of malware does get installed on your machine and starts to transmit data to the Internet.

There are two types of firewall:

- Hardware firewall – If you have a modem or router then you probably have this (see Chapter 7 "Networking" for more information). The modem hides the computer's details, making it invisible from the Internet. It's very difficult for anyone to get round this

- Software firewall – A software application that checks incoming and outgoing connections to your computer

Don't forget

Don't be frightened by all this talk of viruses, malware and inbound attacks. It is a risk of connecting to the Internet. But once you've got anti-virus software and a firewall you're all protected, and what you'll gain from the Internet far outweighs the risk.

98

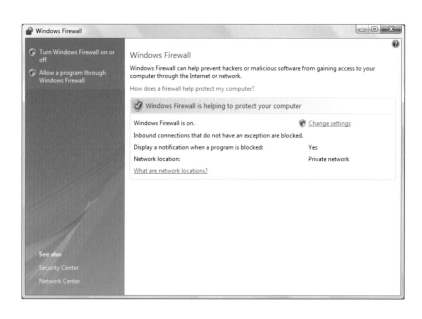

...cont'd

What comes as standard?
Windows Firewall comes as standard in all versions of Windows. It provides a good, reliable firewall, and you can configure how much it does automatically and how much it should check with you.

Mac OS X Firewall, the built-in firewall for Macs, checks for unwanted incoming traffic, but is more limited in other functionality. You should either get technical help to set it up correctly, or invest in one of the other available packages.

Installing a software firewall

1 As part of your initial Mac or Windows PC setup follow the prompts to turn on the default firewall

2 For Windows PCs, decide if you want to use a different firewall. The main reason for doing this would be to enable you to manage all your security settings in one place, for example via an Internet Security suite like McAfee or Norton

3 For Macs, decide if you need to buy a more comprehensive firewall (recommended). Consider a program called Little Snitch

4 Take the time to train your firewall. As programs connect with the Internet, you'll be prompted to confirm that each one is bona fide. This can be difficult to understand, so read each prompt carefully before agreeing.

Cheaper alternatives you could consider:
There are a number of free firewalls you can choose from:

- **Windows** – ZoneAlarm and Comodo, but by preference you should use Windows Firewall

- **Macs** – DoorStop X is a free firewall for the Mac

Don't forget

If you use Internet banking then it's worth asking your bank if they provide anti-virus or security software. Some banks do, because they believe that the better your computer is protected, the safer your money is.

Sending Emails

There are two main ways that you can send and receive emails on your computer:

- Choose a web-based service to read and send email while connected to the Internet

- Download your email to your computer, making it available even when you're not connected to the Internet

Web versus downloading

Companies like Hotmail, Windows Live, AOL, Yahoo! Mail and Google provide websites where you can create an email address for free, and login to read email sent to it.
The main benefit of web-based email (webmail) is that you're not limited to reading your emails at home – you can access them anywhere you have access to the Internet, for example while you're on holiday.

The downside is that all your emails are stored on someone else's server and it's difficult to copy them all to your computer, if you want to keep a copy.

Downloading emails using a software package on your computer means you don't need to be permanently connected to the Internet, and you'll have those emails as long as you choose.

Hot tip

Even if you choose to download your email to your computer, you can still read new email on the web while you're out and about. Most email companies provide webmail access specifically for this purpose. There's also a technology called IMAP, which enables you to read mail in a web account without downloading it. So you can get it in both places!

...cont'd

What comes as standard?

Windows 7 doesn't come with any email software as standard, unless the Windows Live bundle of applications is already installed for you – this contains Windows Live Mail (known in previous versions of Windows as Outlook Express or Microsoft Mail).

Macs come with Mail, an integrated part of Mac OS X. Like all Mac applications, it has a standard interface and menu options.

Using different email software

1 Unless you have specific requirements, start with the integrated email client that comes with your computer (or download the Windows Live bundle for PCs)

2 If you want a package with more features for your Mac, look at Eudora, a long-standing email client, or Entourage, which comes as part of the Microsoft Office for Mac suite

3 For Windows PCs, Outlook is available as part of the Microsoft Office suite

4 Once you've installed your software, you'll be prompted to enter your details to complete the email setup. If you already have an email account then you can import in all your existing mail and settings

Cheaper alternatives you could consider

Thunderbird (from Mozilla) is an excellent email program that runs on both Windows PCs and Macs. It's free, and open source, which means there is a team of people constantly updating and improving it. It also supports add-ons, which are extra features developed by fans around the world.

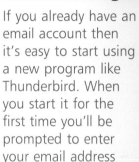

Don't forget

If you already have an email account then it's easy to start using a new program like Thunderbird. When you start it for the first time you'll be prompted to enter your email address and all your emails, settings and address book details will be copied across.

Browsing the Internet

Web browsers are relatively simple applications. They enable you to view websites that people have created. You can do one of the following:

● If you know the web address, type it into the address bar and press Enter or click "Go"

● Type keywords into a search engine, which searches an online index of websites and returns the closest matches to your search term

Some search engines display information from search results straight to you, without you having to go to another website. For example, type "weather Washington" into the search box and you'll get this week's weather displayed in your browser.

All the browsers mentioned on these pages:

● Are easy to use, with a search box customizable to the search engine you want to use

● Keep a history of websites you've visited so you can quickly and easily return to them

● Are secure when you're ordering goods from online sites

Don't forget

Always check for the "secure web site" symbol in your browser before you type in any personal details. It's a yellow padlock icon and is usually found at the bottom of the screen.

...cont'd

What comes as standard?

Internet Explorer comes as standard with Windows.

Safari is the built-in browser for Macs.

Choosing a different browser

Unlike many other software packages, there are very few browsers you need to pay for – the vast majority are freely available and cost nothing to download and use.

Most browsers have been developed to work on both Mac and Windows operating systems – for example you can choose to download Safari for your PC or Internet Explorer for your Mac.

If you want to install an alternative browser then consider one of the following popular alternatives:

- **Mozilla Firefox** (www.mozilla.com/firefox) – like its sister email program Thunderbird, Firefox is an open-source program, which means that it's constantly being updated with new features. It's very efficient and is easy to use. It is available for both Windows PCs and Macs

Beware

Your browser will store copies of some of the web pages you visit on your computer. After a while this cache will cause your computer and browser to slow down unless you clear this space.

103

- **Google Chrome** (www.google.com/chrome) is currently available only for Windows PCs. It has a unique feature – it takes a thumbnail picture of the sites you visit the most and displays them when you open a new tab, so you can quickly get to your favorite sites

Office Tools

A word processor, spreadsheet and database together make up what is known as "office" software, so called because it was originally introduced for workplace computers. Another name for this type of software is productivity tools. But regardless of what you call them, you'll probably need a word processor and spreadsheet application for home use.

A word processor enables you to write and format documents such as letters, brochures and newsletters. A spreadsheet is a document that enables you to format numbers and data, for example to manage your budgeting.

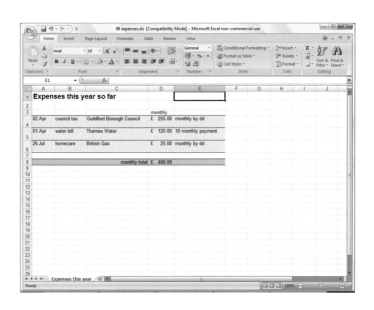

Hot tip

Although it helps, you don't have to buy Microsoft Office to be able to swap office documents with other people. Word processing documents, for example, can be saved as a rich text file (RTF file) format, which can be opened by any word processing package, whether it's Windows, Mac, Linux or any other.

There are a number of options you can choose from:

● Basic text editing software will come with your computer but won't enable you to do more complex tasks, for example, creating and printing labels from your address book or creating spreadsheets

● A more fully featured commercial suite of software will enable you to do much more. It will also come with lots of fun and useful templates for newsletters, invites, posters and much more

What comes as standard?

Windows and Mac each have similar standard functionality – you'll find a basic text editor on both types of machine: WordPad in Windows, TextEdit on the Mac.

A Linux machine usually comes with an open-source equivalent to Microsoft Office as standard, which has basic or mid-range word processing and spreadsheet capability.

Some Windows machines come with Microsoft Works pre-installed, while others come with a trial version of the full Microsoft Office suite. Macs usually come with a trial version of both Microsoft Office for Mac and iWork, the Mac equivalent.

Using different software

1. Consider what you'll be using this software for. Microsoft Office is an expensive purchase – if you're buying a PC with Works included, consider trying Works first, and upgrading later if you find you need specific functionality that's only available in Word

2. Outlook (for Windows) and Entourage (for Mac) come as part of the Microsoft Office suite, so consider this alongside choosing email software

Cheaper alternatives you could consider

- There are a number of open source word processing packages, for example Open Office. These contain programs that are very similar to Microsoft Office but for little or no cost. This is a realistic option if you don't require the more complex features of Word or Excel

- You can try one of the web-based software suites such as Google Documents, avoiding the need for additional software. You simply visit the website where you'll find an online word processor. You won't be able to access this service unless you're connected to the Internet

Hot tip

Microsoft Office is widely used on both Windows and Mac computers.

Microsoft Works is less widely used. Previous versions weren't entirely compatible with Microsoft Office but this has been improved now.

Managing Digital Photos

Once you've downloaded digital photos from your camera to your computer, use photo management software to edit any blemishes and organize and manage the pictures.

Digital photo management software enables you to:

● Download and name files from your digital camera

● Tag the photo with information about the people, location or the event displayed so that you can quickly search for the picture you want

● Make small (or large) edits or changes to the photos, to lighten or darken shots and fix problems like red-eye

Other interesting features in some packages include:

● Built-in integration with websites which enable you to easily publish your photos in online galleries

● The ability to use location information in the photo, added by a GPS-enabled camera, adds your photos to a map of all your photo locations

● The option to edit the images – for example by adding a "Happy Birthday" or other text banner

Beware

Make sure you choose a program that adds your descriptions (tags) to the photo itself, rather than in the software application.

Adding the tags to the photos means they will retain the information you've added, even if they are imported into a different program or web application.

...cont'd

What comes as standard?

Windows 7 doesn't come with any photo management software as standard unless the Windows Live bundle of applications is already installed for you – in which case you'll have **Windows Live Photo Gallery**. This is a basic package that enables you to tag and categorize your photos, and make minor edits, e.g. to remove red-eye.

Macs come with **iPhoto**, which has lots of useful extra features. For example, iPhoto can recognize people's faces. Pick a photo of someone, tell iPhoto who it is, and it will scan the remainder of your photos for that face, adding the name tag to any it finds.

Buying photo software

If you have a digital camera it's worth investing in good software for photo editing and management because of the volume of photos you'll acquire over time. You're unlikely to have the energy to go back and re-catalog all the pictures if you later discover that something didn't work as expected.

Consider investing in **Photoshop Elements** (available for PC and Mac). It's a cut-down version of Adobe Photoshop and it has a professional editing screen in addition to an organizer with advanced features, such as face recognition. Its tagging is logical and very easy to use.

Cheaper alternatives you could consider

- **Picasa** – free photo management software from Google. If you also sign up for a Picasa web photo album account, then you can automatically publish any changes of photos from your computer to the web.

  Check the latest version of Picasa to see whether it stores tag information in photos.

- **Flickr** – an online photo management website that enables you to manage and display your photos to other people. By using this you don't need photo software at all.

Hot tip

Check the photo download options in whichever software package you decide to use, as you can usually change the default photo file name from a meaningless random number to a date, time, number in order taken, or combination of all three.

107

Music and Audio

If you want to manage music and audio files on your computer then you'll need a media player. You won't need to spend any money on this as there are many good, free programs available for both Mac and PC.

Most media players enable you to:

- Play music from CDs and digital music files on your computer and on the Internet

- Create and manage a music library, and synchronize music with a portable digital music player (MP3 player)

- Listen to Internet radio stations

What comes as standard

Windows Media Player comes with all these features and is already installed on Windows PCs.

Hot tip

iTunes and most other media players, can also download and play "podcasts". These are recorded shows, often radio shows, designed to be listened to on computers or digital music players like the iPod.

Use a media player to find podcasts that are interesting to you.

iTunes is the Mac equivalent and comes pre-installed on Macs. iTunes is also available for the PC – anyone with an iPod music player will use iTunes to manage their music.

Alternatives

- **RealPlayer** – used to be a popular media player but has been overtaken by iTunes. Some websites still have music or audio clips in RealPlayer format, but it's usually easier to find the same clip in a standard format somewhere else than to install RealPlayer!

TV and Recording

If you decide to use your computer to watch or record live television then you'll need media center software. This will enable you to:

- Watch and pause live television

- Record television programs, using space on the hard drive instead of a video recorder

- Watch programs, videos or other media files downloaded from the Internet

What comes as standard

Most versions of Windows 7 comes with **Windows Media Center,** a program that lets you watch and record television, listen to music and view photos. It's all within an interface that's designed to work with a remote control, and not necessarily a mouse.

This enables you to have a PC connected to a television without it looking like a computer, e.g. needing a keyboard or mouse.

Don't forget

In order to successfully record television programs you'll need to invest in a more powerful computer, as well as a TV tuner. See Chapter 8, Buy The Right Thing.

109

Mac OS comes with an application called **Front Row** which is an equivalent media center application. You can also use iTunes to play video files, but look at **EyeTV** (ElGato software) if you want to record live television.

Web Publishing

Creating a website is something that many seniors want to do, sometimes for business, but mostly for pleasure. Today, it's easier than ever to get online. With the large number of free blog and photo sharing websites, you rarely need a traditional website design software package.

Many people use websites like **Wordpress** (www.wordpress.com) or **Blogger** (www.blogger.com), which contain ready-made templates – you simply add your text, photos and web links and you're online! You can even customize the colors and design of the pages for your account.

Hot tip

If you don't want to learn a new program but want to publish a blog, you can create a blog post from within Microsoft Word. Click on the Windows button, and choose New Blog Post.

For publishing albums of photos online, consider a site like **Flickr** (www.flickr.com), which enables you to load a large number of photos to an account that's personal to you, and share the photos with other people. Some people also use **Facebook**, a social networking website, to store photos.

Alternatives

If you do want to create complex web pages, then Macs are definitely the winner in this category. **iWeb** comes pre-installed on all Mac computers. It's easy and quick to use: simply drop in pictures, type in text and move all the items around until you've created your ideal web page.

You'll need space on a web server to put your pages – you'll need to find out more if you want to publish web pages.

Web-based Services

You'll find that there are lots of programs and services that are web-based. Instead of installing large programs onto your computer's hard drive, the program provider stores the software on a website for you to use (although you will occasionally need to download a small piece of software, depending on the service).

Benefits of web-based services include:

- Not needing to download or install large software files onto your machine

- Always having the most up-to-date version of the software because it's updated by the provider

However, you won't be able to access these services at any time that you don't have an Internet connection.

Online music
Spotify is a website that enables you to play tracks from pop and classical music albums. It's supported by the record companies involved so there's a wide range of available music. Create an account at www.spotify.com.

Video calling
Skype is a well known online video and telephone service. As we described in Chapter 2, you can use Skype to video call other friends and family with Skype accounts. As well as investing in a web cam, you'll need to create an online account at www.skype.com.

Communications
In this day and age it's very rare to need a fax machine, but if you do need to, then there are online services available, like **Efax** (www.efax.com). Register to get a fax number, to which your correspondent faxes the document. The fax service receives your document, and you read it online.

You can also do word processing online using Google Documents. It's just like a word processor on your computer except it's web-based software.

Beware

The downside to most web-based service is that it needs a good, permanent Internet connection. Check that your connection is suitable before you sign up for the service.

When to Update

Just like all other aspects of computing, software is constantly being changed and improved. New versions of software packages appear just as soon as you've bought an older version! Upgrading paid-for software is expensive – in some cases it can be more than 50 percent of the price you originally paid. So in that case, do you always need to update to the latest version of software?

The answer is generally: it's up to you. Have a look at what changes you'll get for your money, and read reviews of newer versions on the Internet. If you're happy with the software you're using, and you don't think you need a new version, then stick with what you've got.

However, it is recommended that you always upgrade in the following circumstances:

1 If the upgrade has been issued because there are problems with the existing software package, e.g. there are security issues or bugs that need correcting. These updates should be free

2 If the software is related to the security of your machine, i.e. the anti-virus, firewall or operating system. You should generally always have the latest version of this software

3 If the support for a product will be void, or run out, if you don't upgrade

Always shop around for the best price. In addition to computer stores, you'll find software on sale in bookshops, stationers and supermarkets, among others.

The only reason not to upgrade free software is if you're worried about the new version working on your system, or if it's a beta version and you're worried it might be unstable.

Don't forget

Anti-virus software has two different update cycles: the library of viruses usually updates every day, so that you're always protected against the latest viruses, while the security software itself only needs updating a year or more apart.

7 Networking

Networking your computer enables you to get all your purchases working together, as well as to access the Internet.

Networking Essentials

It's quick and easy to set up a home network by connecting together different parts of your computer equipment. The main reasons for doing so are to:

- Get all the different bits of your computer equipment, e.g. computer, printer, scanner and any other devices, to work together

- Provide you with Internet access, so that you can make the most of the Internet: visit websites, send and receive emails etc.

If you have multiple computers in your home then a network will also:

- Enable multiple computers in the household to share files, e.g. a central store of family photos or contact information

- Provide access to a single printer or scanner from all the computers on the network

- Make the Internet connection available to all the computers in the household

Temporary visitors can use the network too, so if family members visit with a laptop, they can access the Internet without having to use your computer or disturb your connections.

This chapter gives you all the information you need to set your computer up at home, as well as an explanation of the different Internet connections you can choose from.

Hot tip

Most networking equipment comes with instructions and a step-by-step "wizard" interface, which makes it easy to install without technical support.

See Chapter 4 "Peripherals" for more information about how to connect devices to your computer, including printers, scanners, multimedia devices and digital cameras.

Chapter 4 also shows you the different cables that are commonly used to connect devices.

A Home Network

There are two common networking methods: wired and wireless. There are advantages to both methods; each uses slightly different hardware equipment.

Internet Modem

Ethernet Adapters

Router

Wireless Adapters

115

Beware

There are a number of different wireless technologies. The most common are: Wi-Fi, usually used to connect your computer to the network; and Bluetooth, which connects computer devices to each other in order to transfer data between them.

Wired networking

This works by connecting different devices together using cables and connectors. This gives you the most reliable connection but does limit where you can locate your computers and peripherals, such as printers, as the cables need to reach between the different units.

You'll need to have the computer close enough to plug into the Internet access point. This is usually a router or modem and it's normally connected to the phone line or cable line.

So you're additionally limited to having the computer near to where the phone line enters the house.

...cont'd

Wired technology

Wired networking is based on a technology called Ethernet, however the components and adapters are referred to by a confusingly large number of different names. You may hear any of the terms below used to refer to Ethernet wired networking:

- Ethernet; Ethernet adapter

- Network Interface Card (or NIC)

- 10BASE-T, 100BASE-T or 1000BASE-T

- RJ45 connector

- Twisted pair

The generic term "network cable" usually refers to an Ethernet cable with an RJ45 connector at each end. It looks similar to a phone lead but with a larger connector.

Don't forget

The main difference between the wireless versions – B, G and N – is speed. B refers to the older and slower equipment, while N is the newest and fastest. In practical terms, G or N will work equally well for home users.

116

Wireless technology

It's a similar situation with wireless – the following terms all refer to the wireless technology used for home networking:

- Wireless or Wi-Fi

- 802.11b; 802.11g and 802.11n

- Wireless G; Wireless N

Desktop Requirements

The best way to network a desktop computer is to put a network adapter into it. Desktop machines generally have plenty of expansion space and putting the adapter inside prevents it from getting knocked. Internal adapters also have the fastest data transfer speeds.

You can get internal adapters that either take a cable or have a wireless antenna to connect to a network. Some computers come with built-in adapters, so check this before you buy one.

Got an adapter?
Many desktop computers come with adapters fitted as standard, but if yours doesn't, then you have a few options to choose from.

1. Check to see if your computer already has an adapter installed. Check the unit and any documentation that comes with it

2. Request an adapter as part of ordering the machine, although this depends on where you buy it from

3. Find a computer support specialist to install one in your computer for you

4. Use a USB network adapter you can install yourself. Read on for more information about this option

Laptop Requirements

Most laptops come with both a wired and wireless adapter built-in. This is because the computer has very little expansion space so the components are added at the time of manufacture. In addition, the portability of a laptop means that it is more likely to need a wireless connection than a desktop computer, so this is also included at manufacture.

However, if you have chosen a laptop that doesn't have a network connection, then you can easily add a wireless connection to your laptop. There are a couple of options you can choose from:

1 Firstly, check that you don't already have a wireless connection option. Some laptops have a physical button on them to activate/deactivate wireless; others require you to choose an option onscreen

2 If you have an empty slot on your laptop (known as a PCI card slot) then you can buy a Wireless card to insert there

3 Alternatively, you can use a USB wireless adapter that will fit into any standard USB connector on your laptop

You can use this same USB adapter on a desktop machine if required: simply plug it in to any free USB slot on the machine. This is a viable option if you don't have a wireless network adapter and you don't want to add an internal adapter.

Beware

Macs have all the same features albeit with different names. The wireless network feature on a Mac is called "Airport".

Multiple Users

If you want a number of people to have access to a single computer, you can create a user account for each person.

A user account, or profile, enables you to save settings that

are specific to you, including background wallpaper, file locations and shortcuts, web browser bookmarks and email settings. Each person logs into their profile with a user name: passwords are optional.

The screenshots on this page show how this works on a Windows PC but the same functionality is also available on a Mac.

As well as a name, you can additionally assign a picture or photo to each user account.

If any of your users are children then you can enable Parental Controls for those accounts, which lets you restrict what programs or games the user is allowed to access, what websites they can browse, and even the time of day they are allowed to log on.

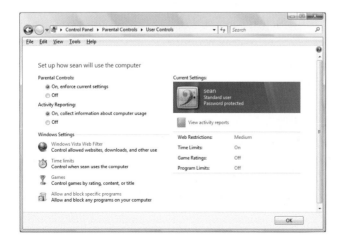

Don't forget

There is a lot of information on the Internet that is not suitable for children and it's difficult to keep an eye on them all the time. Use the parental controls to help manage what they can access.

File Sharing

Whether you want to share files with another user on the same machine, or with another computer on the network, it's easy to set up.

This can be enabled in both Windows and Mac OS, although Windows makes this particularly easy:

1. Make sure there's a user account for the person you want to share documents with

2. Highlight the folder you want to share and click on the Share button in the top ribbon. Alternatively, right click on the folder and choose Share...

3. Select the correct user from the dropdown list and click on Add. Choose the permission level you want them to have: **Reader** (they can't make changes to the files in the folder), **Collaborator** (the user can make changes to files but can't delete them), or **Co-owner** (the user can edit or delete files in the folder, as well as create new files)

If the user is on a different computer, you can send them a link to the folder that you've shared.

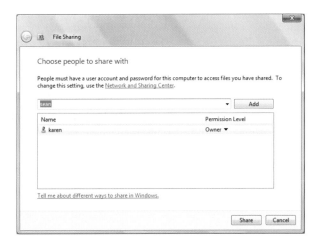

Internet Access

Networking your computer will enable you to get access to the Internet. The most common connection is a "broadband" or high-speed connection, usually provided by your phone or cable provider.

However, high-speed connections are not available everywhere – check with your provider before you sign up.

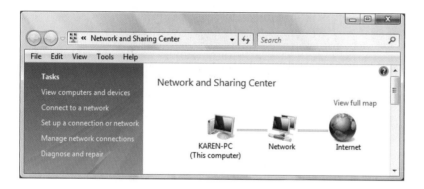

Understanding connections

Whether you're using your computer to look at a website, read a document, send an email or watch an old television program, data is passing through your connection from or to the Internet.

The speed at which you can download and send data, i.e. get it from the Internet onto your computer or vice versa, will vary depending on the following factors:

- What type of Internet connection you have (covered in the next few sections)

- Where in the country you live – both for the quality of the cabling in your local area, as well as how far away you are from the local telephone exchange. The further you are from the local exchange, the slower your connection will be

Beware

Security can be an issue on wireless networks. Make sure you follow the instructions or get someone to help you.

The biggest issue is people nearby using your Internet connection remotely. You'll find that your connection is slower, and they aren't contributing to the monthly charges!

Internet by Phone

122

Don't forget

Make sure you get the right modem. If you're using your phone line then you'll need an ADSL modem.

ADSL stands for asynchronous digital subscriber line. In short, it's the technology that uses a phone line to transfer data.

The most common type of broadband connection uses your existing phone line. Internet traffic and phone traffic are carried at different frequencies on the line, so your phone is unaffected by Internet use – you can ring out and people can ring in as normal while you're using the Internet.

To enable this you will need to:

1 Ask your telephone service supplier to activate your phone line to carry data signals as well as phone calls. There's no physical work required to do this, but you will usually need to pay an activation fee

2 Plug a signal splitter (also known as a micro filter) into your telephone socket, which enables you to plug in a telephone and modem at the same time

3 Connect your computer to an ADSL modem, which plugs into the phone line. Some phone suppliers provide this as part of signing up to their broadband package: you'll need to buy one if they don't

Hot tip

You'll also hear the modem referred to as a "router". Technically a modem is different to a router, but as most home units are a combined router and modem in a single box, it doesn't really matter what you call it.

This broadband connection is usually paid for on a monthly basis. Some providers have rules about how much data you can download each month before you are charged extra. In practice you have to be a very heavy user before these come into effect.

Internet by Cable

If you live in an area that has a cable communications provider, then you can choose a cable Internet connection.

It works in a similar way to getting the Internet via your phone line except that it's a different technology underneath – cable companies use fiber optic cables to connect to their network rather than the older copper telephone cables.

To enable a cable connection you will need to:

1 Get a cable box installed if you're not yet a customer, or potentially upgrade your existing connection, depending on its age

2 Ask your cable supplier to activate your Internet connection. You may need to pay an additional charge for this even if you already have other cable services

3 Connect your computer to a cable modem, which plugs into the cable connection. You may receive this as part of your package, otherwise you'll need to purchase one

Similar monthly download limits may apply to a cable Internet connection. Check with your service provider for more information.

Beware

A modem is the device that converts your computer's data into a format that can be sent down the phone or cable line.

If you have to buy a modem, make sure you get the correct type – there are different modems depending on whether you are using a phone line (ADSL) or cable connection.

Other Access Methods

GPRS mobile

Another way to connect to the Internet is using the mobile cellphone network, also known as a GPRS connection (which we cover in the Going Mobile chapter later on).

You'll need a USB adapter, sometimes called a dongle, that plugs into your computer. It looks just like the USB wireless adapter we previously looked at except that it's designed to use GPRS to access the mobile phone network rather than Wi-Fi to access your home network.

As a result, many of these USB adapters are sold by mobile phone companies rather than IT companies and tend to be on a contract basis, just like mobile phones.

Dial-up

This involves plugging your computer into a modem which uses your phone line when required. The modem makes a call to a phone number which connects it to the Internet. You'll need to sign up with an Internet Service Provider (ISP) who will provide you with the phone number.

As well as using your phone line (which can't be used while the modem is in use) dial-up access provides low connection speeds so it can take a long time to browse web pages and download files.

ISDN

In some areas you can sign up for a digital phone line from your phone supplier, called an ISDN line. Because it's digital, your computer plugs straight in to the line.

Internet access via ISDN is roughly twice as fast as using a dial-up connection but it's still considerably slower than a broadband connection.

Beware

Connection speeds are incredibly complicated. If a dial-up modem provides Internet access at a maximum of 56kbps, and ISDN2 provides access at 128kbps you ought to be able to download material from the Internet twice as fast, and so on.

However, some of the bandwidth is used for signalling, plus you may be sharing the phone system cabling with other users. All this results in a lot of confusion and, usually, a connection speed that's slower than you expected.

8 Buy The Right Thing

This chapter looks at the different price ranges that are available to you and gives you an idea of which you should pick based on your needs.

The Process So Far

So far, this book has given you lots of information about computers – what they can do, how they work and the different types that are available.

Understanding the benefits

The first part of the book explained that there are many possible uses for a computer for seniors, and suggested that there are a number of activities that you can undertake with a computer, from activities that are relatively light on computer power (such as "surfing" the Internet or emailing friends and family) to more complex and power-hungry activities, such as photo or video processing.

For those less able to move around, a computer can significantly increase your ability to keep in touch with friends and family outside your home.

Understanding computers

The second part provided you with background information about the components that make up a computer, and explained that you need to understand a little about each part in order to make the right purchasing decisions:

- **The type of computer you choose** – whether it's a traditional desktop, an all-in-one computer, a laptop or a netbook, and whether you choose a Mac or Windows

- **Purchasing other items** – there are other costs you may not have envisaged, such as purchasing items including peripheral devices and any special software you'll need

Knowing what to buy

Continuing on, this part of the book helps you to map your requirements to what's available in the marketplace. It will:

- Explain the different price bands

- Help you to understand what price you should expect to pay for the features and functionality we've been looking at so far

Hot tip

Try using a price comparison website to get an idea of the current prices for different models of computer.

Understanding Prices

There are four main price ranges for computers: budget, basic, mid-range and high-specification. Within each range there are a number of computers from different manufacturers so you'll always have a choice, regardless of what price range you're looking at.

While reading this chapter you should note:

- Apart from the introduction of budget netbooks, the price you'll pay for a computer hasn't changed much since last year. However, the specification of both computers and components has improved, getting you a significantly more powerful machine for your money now

- Prices are given in US dollars and UK pounds. In addition to the exchange rate, the difference reflects the fact that the price of buying a computer in the US is relatively cheaper than in the UK

- Computers are grouped into approximate price ranges. Models that are on the edge of two ranges could be considered to be part of either, so a $700 computer should be considered both as an expensive basic computer and as a cheap mid-range computer

- Price ranges are also approximate because, as we saw in Chapter 5 "Choose Your Type", you'll pay more for the same features if you want them in a laptop or all-in-one computer, or if you choose a Mac rather than a PC

Customization

As well as buying an off-the-shelf computer, you can also choose to customize it by upgrading the existing features or adding more. For example, you could swap the standard hard disk drive for one double the size, for an incremental cost.

Your ability to do this depends on where you choose to buy your computer. It's rarely possible at retail stores (you have to buy the next model up) but can be arranged if you're buying directly from the manufacturer or from an independent.

Beware

If you see two computers that are very similar in name but are at two different stores, it's likely to be the same model underneath.

The Budget Option

If all you want to do is use your computer for basic activities such as send and receive email, visit the Internet, and create documents in a word processor or spreadsheet, then you don't need a powerful computer.

As a result you can get online for relatively little outlay – you can buy a truly budget computer for less than $200 (£150).

While it's an attractive price, you will have very little choice in what you can get for your money. A budget computer at this price will normally be:

- A netbook – which won't be easy to expand or upgrade as it gets older

- From a little-known or no-name brand, with generic software packages, i.e. none of the well known Microsoft or Mac applications

In addition, your computer will have limited features:

- A monochrome screen, which makes viewing photos or other images difficult

- A small disk drive, which limits the space available for storage of larger files, for example photos

- Limited battery life of a few hours (although it will work if it's plugged in)

Hot tip

Search for reviews of machines, particularly when you're buying at the low end of the price spectrum, as many of the manufacturers are not well known names.

Senior issues

As a senior, however, you should seriously think before buying a cheap netbook, as there are other issues to consider:

● Firstly, these netbooks tend to be small, both in terms of the viewable screen area and the size of the keyboard – everything is much closer together and it's difficult to type on them without hitting the wrong keys. As a result, you may find it difficult to use this type of machine

● Secondly, you'll be limited in how much you can expand or upgrade the computer as it gets older, as these cheaper machines are built on a different infrastructure. You can add more storage using a USB connection, but you'll have to go through the whole buying process again if you want to do more than that

● Thirdly, will this option provide you with all of the functionality you require? While it may be tempting to choose the cheap option, is it the right option?

If you really want to get a computer, however, and you have basic needs and very little money to spend, this budget option is a viable way to achieve your goal.

An overview of the budget option

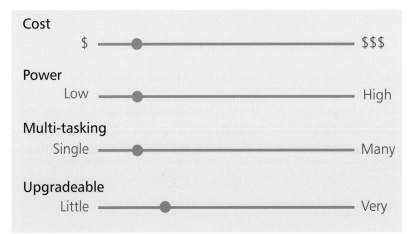

| Cost | |
| $ | $$$ |

| Power | |
| Low | High |

| Multi-tasking | |
| Single | Many |

| Upgradeable | |
| Little | Very |

 Beware

People have been known to buy a full size keyboard, mouse and monitor to use with their budget netbook. If you're tempted, however, add up the costs first. You may find that it's ultimately as cheap to buy a full size laptop or desktop.

Basic Computers

If you want something specific that the budget computer option doesn't provide, for example you want a full size keyboard, a larger screen or a desktop computer; or you have plans that require more processing power, then the budget option is not for you.

Instead, consider the next step up: a basic computer. You can choose from a range of different computers, all of which are suitable for the simple applications like email, Internet browsing and word processing.

Unlike the budget netbook option, a basic computer:

- Comes in a range of sizes and shapes, including desktop, laptop and as an all-in-one unit

- Uses standard software provided by companies like Microsoft and Apple rather than generic equivalents, so you'll have access to support functions like the ability to increase font sizes etc.

- Supports video calling (you'll need a web cam) although you may have only a low quality picture on machines at the cheaper end of the range

- Can store and tag digital photos in a gallery or library, although you'll need a model from the high end of the range for full editing functionality

- Stores and plays digital music

- Has a color screen as standard

- Comes with full-size keyboard and other items

Don't forget that you'll need additional devices for some of these activities. For example, you'll need a web cam for video calling, and a big enough screen for comfortable television watching.

Don't forget

You'll get a full size keyboard with most computers, except the budget netbook options.

Prices start at around $450 (£300) at the bottom end of the range to $700 (£500) for a more powerful laptop or desktop computer.

This description is not exhaustive but should give you an idea of what you can do with a basic computer that you can't do with a budget computer. But for many people, a basic computer is a perfectly viable option that will last them for many years to come.

Upgrading components

If you are broadly happy with the power that a basic computer can provide, but you're concerned about something in particular, then it may be possible to modify that part of the computer.

An example would be if you plan to use your computer to store music files – a basic machine could do this but you might need more hard disk space. In this instance, you could choose to upgrade just the hard disk element of your machine to a larger size.

Your ability to choose this option depends on where you purchase your computer, and we'll cover this in more detail in Chapter 9 "Where to Buy".

An overview of the basic option

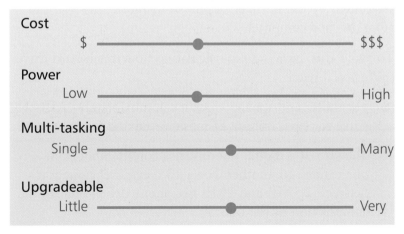

Don't forget

Computers, like cars, mostly come in gray, unless it's a Mac, in which case it's white. You can choose a different color casing but most companies charge extra for this. Check before you buy.

What Basic Can't Do

There are some things that you can't do with a basic computer because it doesn't have the resources required. This includes tasks that require more processing or graphics power – for example, you can't record music or live television.

In some cases the applications just won't work, while in other cases the computer will bravely attempt to perform the tasks. The resulting speed and functionality, however, will be so reduced it will drive you mad before it achieves anything.

Multi-tasking

Because basic computers are limited in processing resources, they aren't generally good at doing more than one activity at the same time. So while you may be fine doing a number of different things, for example surfing the Web or making a phone call over the Internet, the computer will run more slowly if you try to do the two together. In the case of phone or video calls, you'll see a delay or the image will break up, which makes it very difficult to use.

The main issue is that while you can control whether you're doing more than one activity yourself, there are a number of system tasks, for example anti-virus or security updates, that use a lot of system resources and can't be timed.

Hard drive

In many cases you'll find that the most limiting factor for a basic computer is the size of the hard disk drive – you may be limited by the number of photos or music files you can store on your computer.

To avoid this, have a go at calculating how much hard drive space you'll need:

- For music and spoken word it's approximately 1MB of space for each minute of music or talking

- The size of a digital photo varies considerably from one camera to another. For a 10 megapixel camera it's between 1.5MB and 2MB per photo, depending on the composition of the photo

Don't forget

If you want to get on the computer ladder without spending a fortune and the budget option doesn't suit you, then a computer from the basic range is probably what you're looking for.

Start at the lower end of the price range, and work your way up until you find something that suits you.

Mid-range Computers

On top of doing everything a basic computer does, a mid-range computer is designed to cope with applications and software that require more power. You should consider a mid-range computer if you are planning to:

- Edit and process a large number of digital photos

- Watch online films, television you missed, as well as other media files

- Watch live television, (with the right equipment)

- View pictures and videos in high quality picture resolution

- Video calling, with a high quality picture

- Transfer your existing music from tape or record onto your computer

This list is not exhaustive, but gives you an idea of how buying a more powerful machine enables you to do more media-intensive applications.

Prices for computers in this mid-range category generally range from $700–$1,200 (£500–£900) and there is a wide range of makes and models to choose from in this category.

Don't forget

Mid-range computers generally cope much better with media files and multi-tasking. You pay more for a mid-range computer but you get more for your money.

133

An overview of the mid-range option

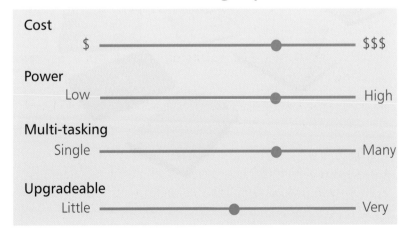

Cost
$ ————————————●———— $$$

Power
Low ——————————●——— High

Multi-tasking
Single ——————————●——— Many

Upgradeable
Little ————————●————— Very

Why Buy a Mid-range?

There are many reasons to invest in a mid-range machine, including:

- You get a more powerful machine, which works faster and will last for longer before it needs upgrading

- You'll get a machine that's better able to multi-task – it won't grind to a halt if you try to use two resource-intensive applications at the same time, or if the computer is running any system processes in the background

- You get a large hard drive as standard, which reduces the need for additional storage later on in the computer's life

- More expensive computers, both desktops and laptops, come with larger monitors as standard

- You're more likely to get additional options as part of your package. For example, you will find a multi-card reader is always bundled with more expensive computers, while some packages include other peripherals, for example a printer or all-in-one printer and scanner

Hot tip

There is very little that a mid-range computer can't do, particularly if you're buying from the top end of the price range.

High-end Computers

This top range of computers is the most expensive, often costing upwards of $1,200 (£1,000), and the computers are usually designed for two main uses:

- Heavy multimedia demands, such as running a home cinema system or television and video recording

- Serious computer gaming – in particular, games that are networked, or have large-screen and fast-moving graphics

The key feature of high-end computers is that they are made from top-of-the-range internal components designed particularly for multimedia applications. They often have additional processing power and memory, which is often assigned specifically for displaying graphics.

Gaming computers are also designed to be more customizable than other home computers. There's lots of space for gamers to add in additional components as they become available.

Gaming computers also tend to have an unusual design or look to them. Some are designed to represent the type of games that are played on them, for example alien-looking cases, and these are expensive to produce. They appeal, however, to the younger generation that tend to play those types of games.

If you plan to use your computer as a media center, then you can choose from a range of multimedia cases designed to fit in with your lounge – it enables you to choose a computer that looks more like a piece of entertainment equipment than an office computer.

Don't forget

The different price ranges do overlap slightly, so there are some machines at the top of the mid-range that could cost as much as a cheap high-end computer.

A Summary

If you're still not sure what computer you should be getting or how much you should be paying for it, here's a quick guide. It lists common requirements, along with the price range and styles of computer that are most appropriate.

This is only intended as a rough guide, and is based on average use – if you know that you'll be traveling often but we've suggested a desktop, then clearly you should consider a laptop too!

Quick requirements guide

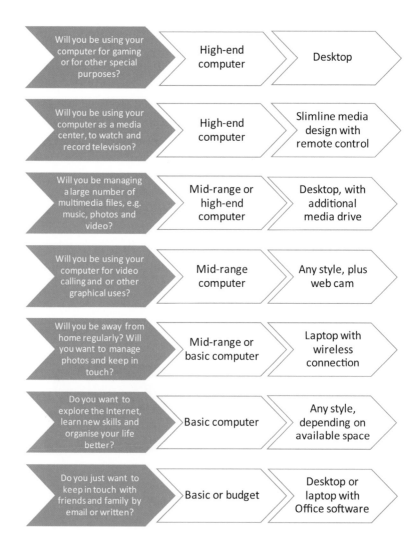

Will you be using your computer for gaming or for other special purposes?	High-end computer	Desktop
Will you be using your computer as a media center, to watch and record television?	High-end computer	Slimline media design with remote control
Will you be managing a large number of multimedia files, e.g. music, photos and video?	Mid-range or high-end computer	Desktop, with additional media drive
Will you be using your computer for video calling and or other graphical uses?	Mid-range computer	Any style, plus web cam
Will you be away from home regularly? Will you want to manage photos and keep in touch?	Mid-range or basic computer	Laptop with wireless connection
Do you want to explore the Internet, learn new skills and organise your life better?	Basic computer	Any style, depending on available space
Do you just want to keep in touch with friends and family by email or written?	Basic or budget	Desktop or laptop with Office software

9 Where to Buy

These days you can buy computers from a huge variety of sources. Where is the best place to look? Who can you trust to give you the right information? This chapter describes how to choose the right place to buy your computer.

Introduction

Buying a computer is similar to buying a car – it's only when you start looking that you realize just how many options there are!

Over the last few years computers have become mainstream. Where previously you had to go to a computer store, or use a specialist mail-order company, you can now buy computers from many different places. You can pick one up as part of your weekly shop in your local supermarket, or buy one from an Internet shopping site, with delivery to your door.

A common mistake with first-time computer buyers is simply to buy the cheapest computer around. We covered earlier in the book why this may not be the best decision, depending on what you plan to use your computer for.

This chapter explains why cheap is not necessarily best for other reasons – there are a number of important factors you ignore at your peril.

Follow these key steps

To help you decide where to buy your computer, we cover the following steps in more detail in this chapter:

Don't forget

You're the one in charge of buying a computer. Don't let pushy salespeople convince you to buy anything you're not sure about.

1 Ask for recommendations of places to go from anyone who has recently bought a computer

2 Note any customer reviews you see about different shops and manufacturers' websites used to purchase

3 Look at what is available in the different outlets, including online shops if you have Internet access

4 Decide which outlet best meets your needs in terms of range of goods, pre-purchase guidance, delivery, support and warranty options

5 Buy that computer. Go for it!

Researching the Options

Recommendations

Computing is an increasingly popular pastime for seniors, regardless of age or previous occupation. So chances are that some of your fellow seniors will have already been through this same buying process.

Talk to people in any organizations you belong to; find out if they bought a computer recently. Talking to local friends and groups will enable you to assess what's available locally.

Also consider younger people, friends or family; many will be up-to-date on the latest technology and places to buy, as they are permanently on the look-out for an upgrade!

Reviews

It's good to do as much research as possible before you spend time visiting different stores. There are a number of different places you can go to get information:

- Consumer associations like Which? in the UK, Consumers Union in the US or the Consumers' Association of Canada, provide reviews of technology, shops and buying practices. Contact your local society for more information

- Buy this month's computer magazines as they often contain a buyer's directory, and customer reviews of different makes, models, components and shops

- You'll also find relevant articles in the technology supplements of national newspapers and magazines

- Societies for older people often provide fact sheets on buying a computer. These societies include Help the Aged and Age Concern in the UK, and the American Association of Retired Persons in the US

Your local library will subscribe to any number of the publications and books mentioned above.

Hot tip

You can save quite a lot of money by reading reviews from publications at the library, as well as using the Internet.

...cont'd

Researching online

The best place to find reviews of shops and service is often the Internet, because people from all over the country post reviews of their experience.

- **Official review websites.** These are sometimes partner websites of computer publications, which means they have a large number of reviews and are impartial

- **Personal reviews**. A number of sites, including Amazon, host reviews against the products they sell. In addition, you'll find a lot of people review their experiences in their personal blogs

Type "computer reviews" in to a search engine and you'll be shown reviews that are local to you.

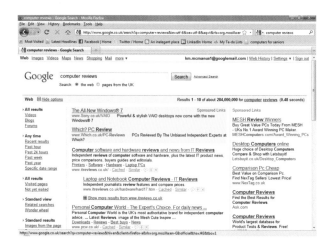

Don't forget

Blogs are online diaries and are useful for gauging opinions on products and services. Many people put their opinions online in a blog.

Blog entries appear in search engines, so search for a make or model or shop name and see what comes up.

Price comparison websites

A comparison website searches lots of different websites and shows you where a computer is available and at what price. Some of the bigger sites provide user reviews from the people who have bought these items.

Beware. Because these sites are maintained by third parties, it's always best to check with the shop or website linked to, rather than rely entirely on these sites.

Availability and Delivery

Different outlets will have drastically different timescales for the availability and delivery of your computer. For example, if you want to collect a computer so you can go home and immediately set it up then you should go to a shop with stock, rather than buy online.

Availability and payment

In most cases you will have to pay up front for your computer, whether you take it away there and then or have it delivered a month later.

Some larger stores do offer "buy now, pay later" financing deals. Look for the 0% interest deals to avoid paying over the odds for your machine.

If the model you want is in stock, you'll be able to buy and take it away on the same day. Otherwise you'll have to keep checking stock availability and return to the store when there are more in stock. Not all stores provide home delivery.

Delivery

If you're buying your computer online or by phone, then it will be delivered to your house by courier. In most cases you'll pay an additional charge for delivery, even if there's no other option, so account for that in your budgeting.

If you're concerned about your ability to handle a large or heavy machine then consider home delivery. You'll still need to move the computer around at home, but you can unpack the boxes in your entrance hall and take items one at a time.

Note the following points:

- Some companies, including Apple, waive delivery charges for larger purchases

- If there's a computer you want and it's not in stock in the store, you can sometimes buy it from the company's website, and have it delivered to your home

Beware

Beware of financing deals. A computer doesn't have a very long lifetime, so with some of the longer deals, e.g. 5-year deals, you're still paying off the computer after it's dead and gone!

Support and Warranties

Post-purchase support should be one of the key considerations when you buy a computer and yet many people simply go to the shop that sells the cheapest items.

Although many computers are set up at their destination and then provide years of sterling service, there are always a few that go wrong, whether it's during the initial setup or a few months down the line.

Thinking ahead about the support you need enables you to survive problems later on in your computer's life.

Not all sellers and manufacturers deal with faults in a consistent manner, and the after-sales service you get can vary drastically from one company to another.

After-sales support

Like many large purchases, a computer will come with a statutory warranty (or guarantee) for a fixed period of time from the manufacturer. This means that if your computer breaks or becomes unusable during this time, then the manufacturer has a duty to fix it.

As with all insurance policies, the issue does have to be a genuine problem with the computer – dropping a cup of tea into it, or other accidents, are not covered.

Hot tip

Although accidents to your computer are not covered on your manufacturer's warranty, you'll probably find that your household insurance can be amended to cover this situation. Check with your insurer for confirmation.

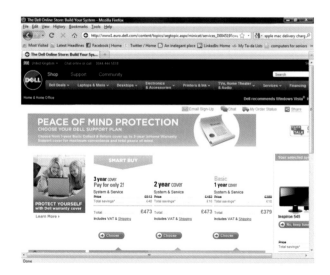

The options: manufacturer or retailer

Most manufacturers attempt to repair the defect in the first instance, usually determining and fixing the fault over the phone. If that fails, an engineer from the company will look at the computer, either on site (i.e. in your home) or at the company service center, depending on the warranty or support option you have chosen:

- **Return to base**. You'll need to pack the computer back into its box, with all the accessories, and arrange for a courier to pick it up

- **On-site or at home**. An engineer will come to your house to look at the problem. This usually costs more

If you're buying from a retailer, rather than directly from the manufacturer, some also offer their own support in addition. Depending on the store, they may provide their own telephone support line or have engineers who will help.

It's worth shopping around for the best support deal on offer. Murphy's Law says you'll regret it if you don't.

The options: local support

Packing up the computer to return to the manufacturer can be a tiring option. So instead consider what support you have locally.

- Local independent computer stores are particularly good for this – and it's easy to get recommendations from people you know

- You may have a younger family member who knows about computers, although you should only rely on this if they are close enough to be able to come round when you need them. It doesn't work if they live three hours drive or a country away

Local support does enable you to spread the cost of post-purchase support by arranging for any additional help at the time it's required, if at all.

Don't forget

Check the phone number that you would need to use to call for support – some companies provide toll-free numbers, while others require you to ring an expensive national number.

143

Computer Warehouses

On every large out-of-town trading estate in the world there is a computer warehouse. Whether it's called PC Mart, PC Heaven, or PCs 'R' Us, they're all very similar – a building built like an aircraft hangar, full of computers, peripherals, software, ink, paper, games, manuals and so much more.

This is not everyone's ideal shopping environment, but there are advantages to shopping in a superstore like this:

- **Big range of makes and models.** Warehouses tend to have computers from a wide range of different manufacturers

- **Lots of computers on display.** You can stroll around at your leisure, looking at the different types and pressing the keys to see how they feel

- **A large stock room**. There's a good chance the one you want is in stock, so you can take home anything you buy

- **Wide range of other products.** You can also get a good idea of what printers, scanners and other hardware is available, as well as software, consumables such as printer cartridges, and related books

- **Staff that are used to lifting boxes.** There are usually a good number of people to help you get your purchase to your car. They are used to being asked to help

Beware

Continuing the tradition started by television shops before them, monitors in these large stores are rarely set up correctly (or have been fiddled with by too many visitors). This can make it difficult to judge what the picture quality is really like.

Disadvantages of computer warehouses include:

- **Variable staff knowledge.** Because of the sheer volume of equipment on display, it's difficult for staff to know about everything on display. And if you're a novice, it's difficult to tell if the person helping you really knows what they are talking about

- **PC bias.** These stores are traditionally PC stores, and although they do sell Apple and Mac computers, the range is often limited, and certainly won't be as large as that of a dedicated Apple shop

- **Post-purchase support.** Like many larger stores, research in the UK has shown some warehouses don't tend to do as well in customer satisfaction surveys for after-sales product support

- **You need a car.** Most stores are located outside of towns and may not be easily accessible on public transport

Beware

Although many of these superstores advertise their in-house technical support teams, these experts are usually part of the after-sales team, working on broken computers rather than walking the floor to answer questions.

Top tips for shopping in a superstore

1. Take the opportunity to work on the computers, so you can see what they look like, how the keyboard feels, etc. Find a sales assistant to help you if the computer is turned off or the screensaver is active

2. Ask the sales assistant how long they have worked in this shop, and talk to them about what computer they have themselves at home. This gives you an idea of how much experience they have

3. Don't allow yourself to be pressurized into making a decision there and then. Make notes about what you've seen and like, and go home to consider all your options

Department Stores

Many people prefer to buy electrical equipment from traditional department stores, usually because the ethos of the shop is different – many of them have retained the high levels of customer service that were instilled in them during their time as family-owned companies.

A common misconception is that it's more expensive to buy goods in department stores, but this is often not the case.

The advantages of shopping in a department store include:

- **Well trained staff.** Staff tend to specialize in a particular department, enabling them to become more highly educated on their wares

- **Good support.** Many department stores provide their own after-sales service in addition to that provided by the equipment manufacturer

- **Easy to reach.** Many department stores are in the town center or city center, making them easy to reach by public transport

- **Use your existing store card.** You can continue to get any preferential shopping rates, as appropriate

Disadvantages of department store shopping:

- **Limited in-store stock.** Smaller stores may not stock very many computers

- **City center location.** It's more difficult to pick up your computer, which may result in you having to pay a delivery charge

Even if the prices are more expensive, you may still prefer to buy at a department store if it's your favorite store.

Support – both during the buying process and after you make your purchase – is a key part of buying a computer.

Supermarkets

It has recently become common to see a fully boxed computer set sitting on a shelf in your local supermarket, normally located somewhere between the crockery and the fruit and vegetable sections.

While it may not have been your first thought, there is a definite place for supermarket computers, but it does depend on the actual model of computer that's for sale:

- You won't get much choice. Generally supermarkets stock a small range of models

- The models in stock are usually at the cheap end of the market, and therefore are less powerful machines

  This is presumably because a purchase costing hundreds of dollars or pounds sticks out in a shop selling tins of beans in cents or pennies

So check the available computers carefully to see if it's a model that will actually meet your needs, as we discussed earlier on in the book.

If it is, then there are definite advantages to buying it from a supermarket:

- You get a large number of loyalty club points

- It's easy to pick the computer up from the store as it's both nearby and generally has plenty of parking

Buying online
If you don't have a car then you can still benefit from the loyalty club points without having to pick up a unit from the store.

Many supermarkets have an online shopping site that enables you to purchase furnishings, clothing and electrical equipment in addition to your weekly shopping and have it all delivered to your front door. You may need to pay a delivery charge in this instance.

Beware

Because computers are not in a supermarket's key product range, the computer may not offer such good value for money as one bought from another supplier. Check around before you commit to a supplier.

Independent Retailers

Most towns have an independent computer store, usually set up by someone local who knows about computers. If the store has been around for any number of years, then you can be pretty sure that it's a reliable option, because the people that run them rely on skill and good business to continue living and working in the local community.

Contrary to popular belief, smaller stores are not always more expensive. You may not always find the same wide range of well known brands but you'll usually get a fair price.

Advantages of using your local retailer include:

- Your computer is often made especially for you by the shop, which makes it easy and cheap to get that extra large hard disk drive or additional memory

- There is local, ongoing support for your computer. You can usually arrange a home visit, or simply take the computer over in your car

- You can be sure that everyone working in the shop knows about computers, unlike in the larger stores where the sales assistant might be selling computers one day, televisions another

- It's good to support local businesses. If the store is a long standing community business then you know that you'll get good service

Hot tip

Making friends with the staff at the local computer shop is a good idea. Technicians based at a small, independent store are more likely to offer an "in-home" repair service than larger shops.

Other Stores

There are a number of other places you can buy a computer:

Household electrical stores
Electrical goods stores now sell computers, which you'll find amusingly nestled amongst the rows of fridges, washing machines and dishwashers.

These stores stock a smaller number of computers than a computer warehouse and there won't be as many manufacturers represented. But there's usually an entire range of machines covering a wide number of price points.

You may prefer this to a warehouse store – there's a sensible range of computers and, as the shops are primarily a white goods store, there are generally less customers crowded around the different computers.

Airport tax-free shopping
If you're traveling anywhere by plane in the near future, then you could choose to buy a computer at an airport store, where you can get purchases tax free, or at least at a significant discount.

There are sometimes rules in place about what products can be bought and whether you have to take them to your destination before bringing them back into the country which may make it a more appropriate option for the smaller, portable devices. Check with the store in question before you travel.

Hot tip

Shopping for a computer at the airport is a good use of time, unless you have to take your purchases with you on your flight. Check before you fly.

Online Purchases

If you don't fancy going around real shops in your quest to buy a computer, and you have access to the Internet, it's entirely possible to avoid visiting a single shop.

However, even if you subsequently decide to purchase your computer from the Internet, you really should go out to the shops to have a look and try out some real-life computers. It really is the only way to get a feel (literally) for what's out there at the time you're looking.

Advantages of buying online

- You can easily customize the computer you buy, e.g. you can choose to add extra memory or increase the size of the hard disk drive, as the computer is usually built specifically for you

- Good websites prompt you with all the possible options you can choose from, so you won't forget any part of your order

- You'll usually see the cost of the order as you go along, so you can see immediately the effect on the price of adding that extra memory or choosing a larger monitor

- You can usually track the status of your order by entering your order reference number into the website

Disadvantages of buying online

- The larger the company, the longer the order time. You may have to wait several weeks for your order depending on how busy the company is

- It can be difficult to get in touch with the right people if you subsequently have questions about or issues with your order, as these companies' systems are based around the website, not around telephone support

- You have to rely on telephone support in the unfortunate case of issues with the computer – you can't go and stand in front of a salesperson and complain!

Don't forget

There is no substitute for going to a number of different stores and investigating the computers that are available; what price they are selling for; what components and specification do you get for your money.

Direct from the manufacturer

If you know which make of computer you want, then you can choose to buy it direct from the manufacturer, rather than buying it from a retailer. Most manufacturers don't have retail outlets of their own – in this instance your only option is to buy over the phone or using the Internet.

The main advantages of buying direct from a manufacturer are as follows:

● There's often a substantial discount for going direct to them instead of a retailer

● There's a wider range of options as almost any combination of components and other options is possible

● You know that the company is reliable and has extensive experience delivering a large number of computer products

The main disadvantage is that, coming from a retail-focused background, some manufacturers aren't really geared up to do consumer sales. You may not always get a prompt response to your questions or issues.

Beware

Watch out for shipping charges if you're buying online as they can sometimes be ridiculously expensive. Look out for special offers that include free delivery.

151

The Apple Store

Whether you are considering buying an Apple Mac or not, a trip to an Apple store is highly recommended. With branches in major cities throughout the country, and around the world, the stores stock a wide range of Apple computers and other digital devices.

All the shops are very modern in design and there are samples of all the different Apple computer models available to view and trial. You can see demonstrations from experts and you can attend regular free sessions where you can learn about different technologies and software packages.

The advantages of buying from an Apple store:

- **Excellent staff knowledge.** Everyone working for Apple is a fan and owns at least one

- **Biggest range of Macs.** You'll find Mac computers for sale in other shops, but the biggest range by far is available in the Apple stores

- **Test all the different models.** The computers are set up for normal use, including with Internet access, so you really can try them with everyday tasks

Buying "Not New"

If you want to save money, you could consider buying a not-new computer. There are three main ways to do this:

Choose a refurbished computer
Many manufacturers and retailers offer this as a way to resell computers that were returned to them with minor faults, which they have successfully fixed. In the meantime, their original owner has either received a refund or had a replacement machine.

This is a viable option to get a reduced cost machine, but you should only consider it if the manufacturer provides an enhanced warranty for the machine.

Before committing to buy a refurbished machine, consider how important reliability is to you. How would you cope if the machine went wrong again?

Buying a second-hand computer
Although computers are available second hand from shops and from Internet sites like Ebay, think carefully before you buy a used computer from a person you don't know. The main issues are that:

- Until you receive the machine you will have no way of telling if the description was correct or if it's a good choice for you

- Unfortunately not all sellers on these sites are reliable. Not everyone receives the goods they've purchased

A more reliable way to get a second-hand computer would be to get one handed down from a friend, colleague or other acquaintance.

But even then, look carefully at the specification of the machine. Many people get rid of a computer when it is no longer fit for their purposes, and if it's no longer suitable for them, will it be suitable for you either?

You might be better off putting the money towards a brand new computer instead.

In Summary

Buying a computer is not just going to the nearest store and picking from what's available. You need to think about the options that are available to you and prepare as much as possible – getting recommendations and reading reviews is key:

- Use the Internet to find out more: you can get online at your local library if you're not yet connected at home

- Read independent reviews of computers and shops: try your local consumers' association or read the current issues of computer shopper magazines

A common mistake with first-time computer buyers is to simply buy the cheapest computer they can find. We've already discussed why this may not be the best technical decision – you risk getting a computer that won't do everything you want it to.

This chapter explains the other reasons for making an informed decision about where to buy your computer.

Who to buy from

There are a growing number of outlets which will sell you a computer, each with their own level of knowledge, care and support. Consider which outlets will best help you by:

- Providing an appropriate level of shop-floor knowledge and support

- Delivering your purchase in a timescale that you'll be happy with

- Making it easy if you need post-purchase support, including warranties and guarantees

Combined with the fact that each outlet stocks a different range of computer, the decision you make about where to buy a computer is as important as the decision about which make and model you will buy.

10 Getting Set Up

Once you've got your purchase home, take the time to set it up properly. The time you spend doing this will be well spent and will prevent problems in the future.

Your Workspace

Don't waste all the time and effort you spent getting a computer that is right for you: make sure you set it up somewhere you'll be able to use it easily and sensibly.

Spend some time setting up your desk and workspace so that the time you spend on the computer will be enjoyable and safe.

Beware

Be careful when moving larger computer parts, e.g. screens and main units. Many screens and components are heavier than they look. Try to avoid moving things on your own, and unplug everything before you start.

Following these key points will help you to work on your computer without straining your body, particularly your back, neck and arms:

1 Find a good chair, preferably an office-style chair or other straight-backed chair. If you don't find this comfortable, try positioning a cushion between the bottom of your back and the chair

2 Make sure you have enough desk space for everything around you. Don't forget you'll need enough space to have work and papers around you as well as the computer

3 Try moving all the components around until you find a configuration that works for you. For example, try moving the keyboard until it's in the right place for your wrists, or use a wrist support

4 Adjust the screen to suit you. Use the contrast, brightness and color adjustment buttons to find the combination that works best for you. Move the screen if there is light reflecting from it, to prevent strain on your eyes

5 Use the accessibility features in the software that your computer runs. For example, make the default font and icon size larger, or use text narration, so that you don't have to strain yourself

6 Take regular breaks from the computer. It's easy to get immersed in what you're doing, but make sure that you don't spend long periods of time doing the same activities.

What to do if you get pains

Sometimes even experienced users get aches, pains or headaches from using a computer the wrong way. It's not serious if you address the problem as soon as it occurs. Start by trying one of the following:

- **Come back later**. Stop using the computer and take a break. Move around and do something completely different before coming back

- **Adjust your equipment.** Move your keyboard and monitor into a different position that works better. Keep trying different setups until you find the one that works best for you

Don't forget

If short cables are preventing you from putting your computer in an optimum position, invest in a USB cable hub. Plug one end into your computer and sit the hub end on your desk – into which you plug all your cables. It means the cables don't have to reach as far and, if you have a tower unit, you don't have to scrabble around on the floor to plug the cables in!

157

Positioning Your Computer

If you've bought a desktop or tower computer, then you should choose a permanent placement for it, e.g. in a separate office or at a desk that will not be put away on a regular basis.

Tower units under the desk should not get in your way – there should be enough space for you to put your feet flat on the floor and to have your chair close to the desk.

Position the screen a good distance away from you, and move the screen if glare is reflecting upon it.

Put the mouse, keyboard and other components you'll be using, on the desk. Make sure you can use the keyboard and that there is enough space to move a mouse or tracker ball around comfortably.

Portable computers

Although portable computers can be used out and about, many people choose to buy a laptop for home use because they can prefer to put the laptop away between uses, or they don't have space to keep something permanently set up.

Either way, you'll have to set up your work area each time you get the computer out. Beware the following common problems with laptop working:

- Don't put a laptop on any old surface, whether it's the kitchen work top or a low coffee table in the lounge. If the computer isn't at the right height or distance then you risk straining your back, neck and arms

- Tempting as it may be, avoid using your laptop on your knees on a sofa or armchair. This puts strain on your back – looking down – as well as on your arms, as the tracker pad and keyboard are too close to your body

- If you have an external mouse or tracker ball, make sure you set it up each time you use the computer – don't do without it "just this once"

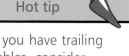

Hot tip

If you have trailing cables, consider investing in cable tubing (similar to hosepipe but split down its length) or cable ties, in order to group together all the loose wires. Both are cheap but effective methods of preventing a nasty accident.

Carrying Your Computer

If you have bought a laptop, then chances are that you're intending to use it out and about. If so, you should carry your laptop or portable computer in a padded bag to protect it from damage.

But this, plus any extra equipment you have, may make your laptop heavier than you expected, so the standard one-shoulder carry bag is likely to cause you discomfort and strain your back and shoulder.

If you intend to travel regularly with your laptop, you should seriously consider buying a rucksack or mini-case with handle and wheels. There are a large number of both types designed specifically for laptops, with extra padding and security locks.

Make sure there is enough room in your carry case for any additional items, for example an external mouse or keyboard.

Beware

If you've bought a desktop replacement laptop, then you should be even more careful about how you carry your laptop around, as it is heavier and larger than the more portable varieties.

159

Other precautions

As with other electrical goods, be careful about how you treat your computer. You should avoid exposing your laptop to extreme temperatures, both hot or cold.

You should also avoid getting your laptop wet – if you're going near water, for example a beach or swimming pool, then make sure it's in a suitable waterproof casing.

Initial Setup

Unless you've paid for an in-house installation service or have family members with the right skills, you'll receive your new computer in one or more large cardboard boxes and you'll need to set it up.

Most computers come part-installed, which means that much of the work has been done for you. But the setup needs finalizing and customizing for you.

Set aside a good few hours to do this. Don't be tempted to rush it – this is important. It's where you set up user accounts and your preferences. Spending time getting it right now will prevent irritating problems later in your computer's life.

You should follow these steps:

1 Unpack all the boxes and check that you have everything you expected. Sometimes items are spread across a number of boxes, so don't panic until everything is open and unpacked

2 Position everything on the desk, checking that the cables are long enough for you to put everything in a position that is comfortable for you

3 Read the "Getting Started" instructions and check if there is anything specific you need to do for your particular installation or setup

4 Plug the machine in, turn it on and follow all the onscreen instructions

Don't start your computer setup unless you've got time to finish it – turning off the computer during the setup process may cause it to fail. The only exception to this is if the computer tells you to, of course.

Beware

Don't be put off by the time it takes to complete the installation. Don't turn the computer off unless it explicitly tells you to.

Completing the Installation

Once you've turned on the computer, you'll be asked to complete all the final details to set up the computer. For a Windows PC, for example, you'll see the following screen:

You'll also be prompted to perform a number of steps, including the following:

1. Choose a user name and password for your computer user account

2. Turn on Automatic Updates, Windows Firewall and other security features to secure your computer

3. Check the clock, time zone and other regional settings are all correct for your location

4. Choose the correct location for your computer, e.g. at home, so that the correct security settings are chosen

Although this is the process for Windows machines, the initial setup is similar for other operating systems.

Beware

You'll need to choose an administrative account user name first of all. This is the master account. Once you've done and installed this, then you can create user accounts for other family members.

Secure Your Computer

If you've chosen a Windows PC then you should check that Windows Updates is set up on your machine. This is a regular update feature provided by Microsoft that you are entitled to as a genuine Windows user.

You should ensure that Windows Updates is enabled and your computer is up to date.

1 Click on the Start menu

2 Type "updates" in the Search box

3 Click on "Windows Updates" under Programs

4 Within Windows Updates, click on Change Settings and check that the option to automatically install updates is selected:

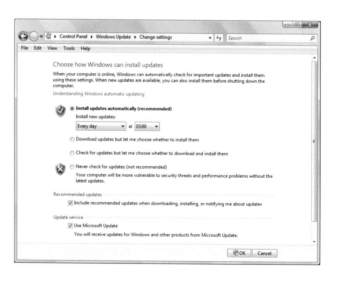

Beware

Macs don't have a direct equivalent to Windows Update, so if you've bought a Mac you won't need to do this. You may, however, be prompted when new updates to the operating system become available.

The updates should download automatically, but you can check at any time using the main Windows Update screen, where you can also download any pending updates.

Prevent Viruses

It's very important that you install anti-virus software before you connect your computer to the Internet. See the Software chapter for an introduction to anti-virus software and the different options available.

Hot tip

Your computer will need to be connected to the Internet to download daily virus updates. If you're not connected, the software will simply try again the next time it detects an Internet connection.

Do the following options in your anti-virus software:

1 Enable daily updates – so that new virus detection information is downloaded every day, to ensure that your software is always aware of the latest viruses

2 Tick the "Scan incoming and outgoing emails" option – to prevent viruses getting onto your machine from other people's emails

3 Set up a time for a regular scan of your computer – to check that nothing has got in unexpectedly

4 Look at the other security options available to decide if they would be of use to you

Protect Your Data

A backup is simply a copy of the data you've got on your computer, stored outside of your computer in case your computer breaks, or you accidentally delete or lose a file. Backups are often made using a CD, DVD, USB key or external hard drive, depending on how much data you have.

Like insurance, it is a protection you should put in place and regularly check, with the hope that you'll never actually need it. Unlike insurance, however, your files will change regularly, so you should be backing up regularly, not leaving it for a year at a time...

Take digital photos as an example. Imagine if all the photos on your computer were to disappear overnight because of a computer or user error. Once they're gone, they're gone, a particularly harsh reality for family photos – it's impossible to turn back time to recapture them.

Backup media options

There are a number of different options for backing up, and some are better than others, depending on your needs:

- Using a **CD** is fine if you don't have much data to back up, particularly if you don't have many photos or other media files

- **DVDs** provide much more backup space per disc, but as a result are more expensive per disc

- At first glance, a **USB key** would appear to be a good device for backup, as it is available in a range of larger sizes than a CD or DVD, and it is reusable. However, while it works well for taking occasional copies of files, many USB keys break or corrupt easily – not ideal for a backup device

- An **external hard drive** is the best option if you can afford one. These are hard wearing disk drives, and come in larger sizes that are much closer to what is required to back up a computer's hard disk drive

Hot tip

Be aware that many types of CD and DVD are one-use only, which means they can't be used again after the first backup. Check carefully before you buy.

...cont'd

Backup programs

You could choose to copy all the files you use to an external disk. However, this is time-consuming and complex – you have to remember to do it, and work out which files need to be copied across. A better option is to use a backup program: Windows provides a built-in backup facility, called the Backup and Restore Center; Macs include Time Machine.

The advantages of using a program like this include:

- You can schedule a regular time for a backup to take place automatically, and if your computer is turned off, or the disk or external drive wasn't available at the right time, then you'll be prompted the next time that you turn the computer on

- Only files that are new or changed since last time are backed up, which reduces the time taken and the disk space required

Hot tip

A backup to disk or CD protects you from your computer breaking but not from the unfortunate events of fire or burglary. This is an added advantage of having off-site backup (for example a web-based service).

Internet-based backup

Another option is to use a web-based service, where your data is copied to a server in a secure location. Some computer manufacturers include a trial subscription with a new computer, otherwise there are a number of companies like iDrive (www.idrive.com). It's easy to set up and works in a similar way to the backup shown above, but there is usually a monthly charge for the storage of your backup data.

Regular Maintenance

There are a number of tasks that you should regularly perform in order to keep your computer working optimally. These are simple tasks to perform and there is minimal risk to your computer, but, if you are at all concerned about your ability to do these, then you have a number of options:

- Get a computer-savvy friend to do them for you

- Buy a "health check" from a computer store

- Ignore them until your computer becomes unbearably slow, then choose one of the above methods for fixing it!

Health checks

This is a service provided by most computer stores. Take your computer into the store, where an engineer will check that everything on it is working as it should be. If anything is preventing the machine from working at full capacity, they will resolve this for you.

The store option is obviously more expensive than doing it yourself, and it's worth checking around because the costs vary greatly depending on where you go. It's also worth checking for reviews of different companies, as value for money also varies greatly from one company to another.

Note that you don't have to go back to the store where you bought the computer. You could choose to use a local computer shop or technician, regardless of where you bought the machine.

Other options include:

- Signing up for an annual support contract rather than paying for a one-off fix

- Choosing to have someone come to your house to fix the issue, which will be more expensive again

Hot tip

There are an ever-increasing number of computer courses available, some specifically designed for senior users. If you'd like to find out more about basic computer maintenance, look for a beginners' course at a location near you.

Top Tips for Health

Here are some top tips for keeping your computer in top working order:

1 Turn your computer off by choosing Shut Down on the Start or Apple menu, not by pressing the button on the main computer unit

2 Delete your Internet cache and history. Each time you visit a website, the browser keeps information about the sites, and sometimes a copy of the page itself. Most browsers have an option to clear the cache, so do this every month or so

3 Empty the Recycle Bin or Trash regularly (right-click on the icon and choose Empty Recycle Bin or Empty Trash)

4 Don't store large files on your computer's desktop – keep them in your personal folders. Windows, in particular, doesn't cope well with very large files on the desktop

5 Run Disk Cleanup (Windows) or Disk Utility (Mac OS X) regularly to prevent problems. These are found in the Accessories or Utilities folder on Windows and Macs respectively:

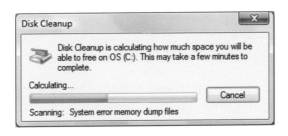

> **Hot tip**
>
> Deleting files from your computer actually moves them in the first instance, to the Recycle Bin, so you can retrieve them if you accidentally delete something. Emptying the Recycle Bin then permanently deletes those files – they're then gone forever.

Sorting Out Problems

If, despite all your maintenance efforts, your computer does go wrong, then there are a number of ways you can attempt to fix the issue:

- Look up the problem online or in a reference guide, and find a solution that you can implement. This is always a good starting point, as something you think is complex or difficult may turn out to have a quick and simple resolution

The Internet is a wonderful resource. Everything that has ever gone wrong is documented there somewhere, along with a solution. Google it!

And if you'd rather take it to someone else to deal with, you'll find reviews of the repair services of local shops and national chains. Check before you book your computer in somewhere.

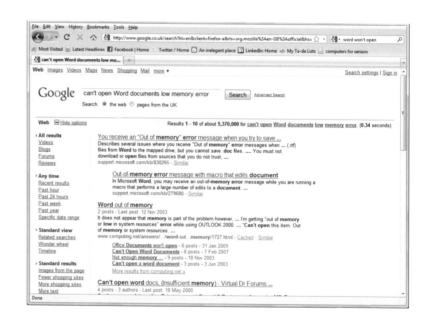

- Contact a local computer technician to solve it for you. Sometimes you'll be able to find a local self-employed technician, or a local computer shop to help you

For more serious issues, you can:

- Take it back to the place you bought it. Although the shop is not liable for post-purchase issues, they may have support staff who are able to help you

- Contact the manufacturer – there may be a warranty on the machine, depending on the options you picked

11 Going Mobile

A mobile device enables you to, among other things, access email and the Internet anywhere there's a mobile phone connection.

Why Go Mobile?

So far in this book we've talked about buying a computer: either a desktop machine for your home, or a more portable computer, like a laptop or netbook, that can additionally be used out and about.

There is another option on top of those we've already discussed – you can choose to buy a mobile device, like those shown below. A mobile device performs a number of computing functions, depending on the model, with the added bonus of being even more portable than a laptop.

Beware

If you're considering buying a mobile device, consider the ongoing usage charges as well as the cost of buying the device itself. These vary considerably depending on the device you buy.

An additional device

The reality is that you are unlikely to choose one of these devices instead of a computer because they are so very small. Their screens can display only a limited amount of information at once, and the keys are the same size (or smaller) than those found on a mobile phone.

You may be interested, however, in looking at a mobile device as an addition to the computer you choose.

As a result, the use of mobile devices is covered in a separate chapter here, rather than as part as of the main decision-making process.

Mobile Technology

Mobile computing started to take off in the late 1990s when two different technologies became much more widely available:

- A number of mobile email devices launched, such as the Blackberry, enabling people to access their emails anywhere there was a mobile network. These devices were mostly used by business users in the early days, due to the high cost of mobile contracts

- Mobile phones started to include a basic web browser so you could view simple web pages on your phone, however the technology was limited at this time – websites had to be written specifically for mobile use. In addition, most phones could only display monochrome colors on their small screens, and they were incredibly slow to use

What's available now?

As the Blackberry developed its phone and media capability, and mobile phones started to incorporate data and email options, the gap between the two camps has significantly narrowed. So all these different types are now simply classed as "smartphones", whether it's a Blackberry, Nokia or Samsung, or even an iPhone. We'll cover these in more detail in this chapter.

All smartphones contain a mobile phone, plus the ability to browse the Internet and access email, but the way they work and the sophistication of the features depend on the make and model.

Hot tip

If you've got an old mobile phone you want to get rid of, donate it to a charity. Look up "mobile phone recycling" in an Internet search engine to find a charity organization near you.

Blackberry

Unlike earlier versions, today's Blackberry is a fully functioning mobile device, providing email access and web browsing in addition to the usual mobile phone, text and picture messaging.

A Blackberry comes with a large full color screen and mini-QWERTY keyboard designed for "thumbing" – typing using your thumbs – although some of the slimline models have a shortened keypad, with two letters per key, which can be confusing when you first start to use it.

172

Some models also include an integrated digital camera and digital music player, which means you only need a Blackberry instead of multiple devices in your handbag.

A Blackberry has its own mini applications, such as a calendar, notepad and to-do list, all of which synchronize with software applications installed on your computer. So you can access your computer's calendar from your Blackberry, and any items added to your Blackberry calendar are transferred to your computer.

The Blackberry is still more commonly found among business users, as the device has a more powerful processor, and it comes with tools and software that enable it to better connect to a corporate network.

Other Phones

An Internet-enabled phone shares many of the same features that we already described for Blackberry: mobile phone, text and picture messaging, web browsing and email access.

The main difference is that there are a large number of phone suppliers, e.g. Nokia, Samsung, Sony Ericsson. So where all models of Blackberry contain the same functionality, phones will look and work differently depending on the make and model.

The main difference is that these smartphones are designed primarily for home users. They are cheaper to buy and run, and there's more of a focus on media applications, such as digital music players, the ability to share information between friends, and access to social networking sites.

Don't forget

Mobile phone tariffs vary a lot depending on a number of factors including: which network you sign up to; whether email and web browsing is included; which mobile phone or device you buy. Check different mobile suppliers before you buy.

Until recently you had to choose a Blackberry if you wanted a bigger keyboard, as most other smartphones have the standard 12-key phone keypad. But other manufacturers are now producing innovative designs. However, the keys are still significantly smaller than a standard keyboard.

iPhone

The iPhone is another make of smartphone, developed by Apple and based on its popular iPod technology. As a result, this particular smartphone is really well designed to cope with digital media, such as music, video and photos.

It's easy to download all those from a computer (PC or Mac) using iTunes, the Apple media player software.

The iPhone also comes with the other features you'd expect: a digital camera, mobile phone, email, web browsing, notepad, calendar and, in some models, map and GPS functionality.

iPhones have touch sensitive screens which are designed to be used with your fingers so, unlike some other flatscreen devices, there is no fiddly pen to lose.

You can "type" by touching the onscreen virtual keyboard – letters displayed on the screen in a QWERTY layout.

Hot tip

A really cool feature of the iPhone is that it knows which way up you're holding it. So turn it longways and the landscape photo or web page will display full screen, or upright for a portrait photo or slimmer image.

iPhone applications

As well as all the standard applications, such as email and web browser, you can download additional "applications" from the App Store. This is an Internet-based shop where people and companies sell applications they have developed, specifically for the iPhone.

Some of the applications put the functionality of the iPhone to great use. In addition to the usual games, you can find:

- A currency converter that's quick and easy to use

- Budgeting application that enables you to type in your expenses – typing them in at the time you spend the money helps you to record accurately what you've spent

- A quick link to your favorite travel timetable site

- Dictionary or foreign language reference guide

175

Some applications are free to download, and you'll have to pay for others, although usually it's only a few dollars or pounds. It's easy to download applications from the store direct to your iPhone.

PDAs

Personal Digital Assistants, also known as PDAs, are another type of mobile device, so-called because they were first developed as an electronic diary and address book – like having a digital secretary, apparently!

These PDAs are the oldest types of mobile device. As early as 1984, Psion launched its first digital organizer – it was huge, gray and looked a bit like a scientific calculator. But later the Psion Revo range was the first handheld computer with a QWERTY keyboard.

Another early PDA manufacturer was Palm, with a device called the Palm Pilot. Palm has continued to develop its PDA into a fully functioning smartphone device. True to its PDA history, the Palm devices have a focus on smart diary and contact management.

For example, you can view a number of different calendars together on your Palm, which is good for people who are still working and have one calendar on their work computer, and another at home.

Handheld computers

As PDAs became more popular, well known names, including many computer manufacturers, such as Dell and Hewlett Packard (HP) started to develop handheld computers. They were usually in a different league – they contained a Windows operating system designed for mobile devices and, as a result, were considerably more expensive.

It's still possible to buy a handheld computer, but beware, they don't have as many features as other mobile devices. For example, they don't all have a built-in mobile phone.

Hot tip

You can often get a wide range of accessories for PDAs, for example a full size keyboard, or mouse/ tracker device that plugs into the side.

Choosing a Device

Having read about all these different mobile devices, you'll see that there is a lot of choice. And while there may have been a great difference between a mobile phone and a Blackberry a few years ago, they have many more features in common now.

So how do you choose the right device for you? Consider the following questions:

1 Do you already have a mobile phone? If so, consider whether you want to learn to use a new model. If not, consider upgrading to a smartphone from the same manufacturer

2 Look at the computer you've bought. Will you (or are you) using iTunes? If so, consider an iPhone

3 Try the devices out first. Choose the make and model you find the most usable, and look at what accessories are available. For example, some devices can be connected to a full size keyboard

4 Look at the amount of money you want to spend and rule out anything that is too expensive. Consider the tariff (see below). For example, a Blackberry is often sold on an expensive business tariff

Choosing a tariff

You will need to join a mobile phone network in order to use a mobile device. You'll usually get charged separately for calls and for data usage or downloads. Email, web browsing and, for iPhone using Apps which connect to the Internet, all count as data downloading.

Depending on the tariff you choose, you will pay for the data you download by amount downloaded, or at a fixed amount per day or month. Choose carefully – otherwise you could end up with huge bills.

Beware

It's possible to buy a mobile device more cheaply if you choose a "refurbished" model. This means that it was returned to the manufacturer, probably with a fault that was subsequently fixed. Check that you'll get the same warranty as for a new purchase before you buy.

Connecting Your Device

Most of the mobile devices we've covered use a technology called general packet radio service (GPRS) to connect to the Internet and send and receive emails.

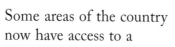

GPRS is a permanent connection, which means you'll receive emails as they arrive, and you can browse the Internet without having to connect each time.

Some areas of the country now have access to a faster technology, called Enhanced GPRS. This is similar, but provides a higher speed mobile Internet access, which theoretically gives you a similar experience to a home broadband connection.

Synchronization

Most mobile devices come with software that you load onto your computer to help manage the transfer of data, including music, photos, files and contact information, between your computer and mobile devices.

In most cases it's easy – simply connect the cable between the computer and your mobile device and the synchronization will start automatically.

Wireless synchronization

Some devices don't require a cable to synchronize with your computer – some use Bluetooth or a wireless network connection instead.

Bluetooth is a form of wireless connection that works only over short distances and is usually used to transfer data between different devices that work together. Another example of a Bluetooth connection would be a mobile phone headset.

Hot tip

You can also use Bluetooth to transfer photos between a digital camera and a computer, if both are Bluetooth-enabled. It's much easier than finding the correct cable each time.

12 Glossary

A definition of the key terms you'll come across.

802.11 – CPU

802.11b/g/n
Official name for the Wi-Fi wireless home networking technology. Each letter refers to a newer and faster technology

ADSL
Short for Asynchronous Digital Subscriber Line. It's the technology used to transfer Internet data down your phone line while still enabling phone calls to take place uninterrupted

application
Another name for a software package

backup
A copy of your data stored outside of your computer in case of emergency

bandwidth
The amount of data that can be transmitted through a connection at any one time. The higher the bandwidth, the faster the connection

base unit
The main component of a desktop computer which contains all the hardware components. A tower unit is a base unit that stands upright, usually on the floor under a desk

Blackberry
A make of smartphone often used by business workers to keep in touch with work email while they're out of the office

browser
An application that enables you to view websites. You can create shortcuts to your favorite sites so you can quickly get to them. Most browsers have a search engine built in

CPU
A term used to refer to a number of different things. See *base unit* and *processor*

Disk Drive – Media Card

disk drive
A storage device for files, which are all kept until you delete them, even if the computer is turned off. CD/DVD/hard disk and USB keys are all types of disk drive

dongle
A USB key specifically designed to give computers access to the mobile phone network for connecting to the Internet

email
Short for electronic mail. The ability to type a message on a computer and send it to another person who is identified by a unique address. This is usually in the format: something@ispname.com

GPRS
Short for General Packet Radio Service. This is the technology used to transfer data using the mobile phone network

graphics card
A piece of hardware that enables you to view pictures and video on your monitor.

hardware
The physical parts of a computer, both external and internal, e.g. the desktop unit, processor, graphics card, memory

Internet
Short for inter-networking. The name for a large group (network) of computers that are connected together, each containing information or services that are available to you to view or access

iPhone
A smartphone produced by Apple. It contains a particularly strong media player for music and videos

media card
Small data storage card usually found in smaller devices, e.g. smartphones, digital cameras

Media Card Reader – Network Adapter

media card reader

Hardware with slots to take a number of different sized media cards

media player

Software designed to store, manage and play media files such as music, spoken word, podcasts and videos

memory

Hardware inside your computer that provides a workspace for processing instructions while the computer is turned on. The more memory there is in your computer, the faster it can process instructions, and the faster your applications will run

micro-filter

Another name for a phone splitter. See *phone splitter*

modem

A hardware device that converts the data on your computer into the right format so that it can be sent down your phone line or cable connection. Phone lines and cable connections work in different ways so you'll need a different modem depending on your connection type. A home networking modem is usually a combined modem/router. See *router*

motherboard

The main piece of hardware in your computer base unit. So called because it's a piece of board (albeit high tech board) and it's the heart of the operation – everything plugs into it

multi-tasking

Refers to both a processor and computer. The ability to process more than one command at once, or to run more than one application at once, in the case of a computer

network adapter

A card that is inserted into a computer to enable access to a network and, usually, the Internet. Network adapters can be for wired or wireless networks, and can be installed inside the computer or plugged into a USB socket

PDA – Search Engine

PDA
Short for Personal Digital Assistant. A type of smartphone which started off as a digital organizer – with an electronic diary and phone book

peripherals
Devices that work alongside your computer, for example printers, scanners, monitors and keyboards

phone splitter
Plugs into your phone socket and contains two sockets: one for the Internet cable and the other for the phone cable. It separates the sounds of the Internet connection from the phone line, which can be distracting during phone calls

processor
The brain of your computer. All the instructions from the different software applications and hardware components are managed here. Also known as a *CPU*

QWERTY
The type of keyboard layout commonly found in the UK, US and Canada, although some symbols are in different places in those three countries

refurbished computer
A unit that was previously returned to the retailer because it was unwanted or broken, but has subsequently been renovated. Usually sold at a discount

router
A hardware device that enables multiple computers to connect together and share resources including printers and Internet connection. A home networking router is usually a combined modem/router. See *modem*

search engine
An index of website information. Use keywords to return links to pages that contain what you're looking for. Examples of search engines include Google, Yahoo and Bing

Skype – Surfing

Skype
A software application that enables you to make a phone call using your Internet connection instead of your phone line. If you have a web cam then the other caller can see you and vice versa

smartphone
A mobile phone or other handheld device that combines a mobile phone with the ability to send and receive email, browse websites, listen to music and view videos

social networking
Finding other like-minded people to connect with online. A social networking site allows you to join interest groups, share information and photos, and meet/chat to people

software
Applications that enable you to perform specific functions with your computer. For example, word processing software enables you to write documents; web browser software allows you to view websites

sound card
Hardware that enables you to hear sound from your computer. You'll also need headphones or speakers

specification (of a computer)
How powerful the computer is. This depends on which components are included inside the main unit as well as the peripherals you use

spreadsheet
A software application designed specifically to deal with numbers, formulas and other data. It's used for budgeting, financial planning, organizing dates and other planning activities

surfing
Using a browser to view web pages or websites. You can click on links to go from one page or site to another

USB – Word Processor

USB; USB cable; USB port

Short for Universal Serial Bus. It's the name for a data transfer technology that's now a standard on all types of computer. Most peripheral devices connect to a computer using a USB cable that connects to USB ports: one on the computer and the other on the device

USB key

Small item that stores data so it can be easily transported from one computer to another. Generally considered to be a replacement to the floppy disk but with significantly higher capacity

warranty

Cover for the computer in case it breaks down or needs repair. This is usually provided by the retailer or manufacturer

web cam

Digital video camera specifically designed for use over the Internet. Used for video calling and for creating videos suitable for use on websites

web page

A screen of information published onto the Internet for people to view

website

A collection of web pages that are linked together, usually with a common theme

Wi-Fi

Another name for wireless home networking technology. See *802.11*

word processor

Software designed to deal with writing and layout, used for writing letters, newsletters, designing invites and posters and much more. Some word processors have more functions and templates than others

Picture credits

Pictures in this book reproduced by kind permission of:

- Advanced Micro Devices Inc: p49

- Courtesy of Apple: pp77, 80, 81, 94, 152, 174, 175

- ASUSTeK Computer Inc: p51

- Belkin International Inc: pp57, 116, 117, 118, 123

- Creative Technology Ltd: pp46, 47

- Canon: pp65, 67, 68, 69, 74, 75

- Dell Inc: pp58, 76, 78, 80, 81, 82, 84, 128, 134, 142

- DSG International plc: pp144, 149

- Kensington: pp55, 63, 86, 124, 159

- Kingston Technology Corporation: pp35, 41, 45

- Logitech: pp70, 71

- McAfee: pp96, 163

- Microsoft pp36, 59, 62, 72, 89, 91, 92, 98, 104, 106, 108, 109, 119-121, 162, 165, 167

- Nokia: pp170, 171, 173, 178

- Palm: p176

- Research in Motion: pp171, 172,

- Ubuntu: p95

- Wacom: p64

- Western Digital Corporation: pp38, 39, 40, 135

- www.sean.co.uk: p110